2004 PO

ONCE
A RHYME

IMAGINATION FOR
A NEW GENERATION

East & West Sussex
Edited by Sarah Marshall

First published in Great Britain in 2004 by:
Young Writers
Remus House
Coltsfoot Drive
Peterborough
PE2 9JX
Telephone: 01733 890066
Website: www.youngwriters.co.uk

SB ISBN 1 84460 584 1

Foreword

Young Writers was established in 1991 and has been passionately devoted to the promotion of reading and writing in children and young adults ever since. The quest continues today. Young Writers remains as committed to engendering the fostering of burgeoning poetic and literary talent as ever.

This year's Young Writers competition has proven as vibrant and dynamic as ever and we are delighted to present a showcase of the best poetry from across the UK. Each poem has been carefully selected from a wealth of *Once Upon A Rhyme* entries before ultimately being published in this, our twelfth primary school poetry series.

Once again, we have been supremely impressed by the overall high quality of the entries we have received. The imagination, energy and creativity which has gone into each young writer's entry made choosing the best poems a challenging and often difficult but ultimately hugely rewarding task - the general high standard of the work submitted amply vindicating this opportunity to bring their poetry to a larger appreciative audience.

We sincerely hope you are pleased with our final selection and that you will enjoy *Once Upon A Rhyme East & West Sussex* for many years to come.

Contents

Barnham Primary School, Barnham

Joshua Kemp (11)	13
Jessica Spain (8)	13
Georgina Denyer (10)	14
Jed Bates (8)	14
Megan Mead (10)	15
Holly Dean (7)	15
Rosie Beller (10)	16
Charlotte Tester (9)	16
Ben Root (8)	16
Declan, Micha Oates, Emily, Charlotte Tester, Dannia, Scot & Jack Spear	17
William Green (9)	17
Emily Rudge (9)	17
Matthew Kerr (10)	18
Jessie Laker (8)	18
Freya Holland (8)	19
Jamie West (9)	19
Aaron Green (9)	20
James Stephenson (8)	20
Zac Rigby (9)	20
Logan Sword (9)	21
George Bathews (9)	21
Nathan Green (8)	21
Dominic Sibun (8)	22
Robert Edward Walker (8)	22
Callum Boxall (8)	22
Kieran Hornsby (8)	22
Emily Golding (8)	23
Blake Brundle (9)	23
Ryan Burch (9)	23
Hannah Ide (9)	24
Millie Hobbs (10)	24
Samantha-Anne Glover (9)	24
Gavin Kerr (8)	25
Luke Elsworth (9)	25
Thomas Paget (9)	25
Declan Pawsey (9)	25
Callum Brundle (11)	26
Danni J Noble (9)	26
Charlotte Edwards (9)	26

Rory Myers (11)	27
Craig Dummer (11)	27
Holly Challinor (10)	28
Shannon Parrott (8)	28
Megan Collier (10)	29
Chelsea Betsworth (10)	29
Grace Pidgeon (9)	30
Bradley Cranwell (11)	31
Louise Chapman (10)	31
Abbie Smith (10)	32
Charlotte Dean (10)	32
Mazharul Islam (11)	33
Billy Court (10)	33
Toby Parry (11)	34
Nathan Hall (7)	34
Kjersti Napier-Raikes (11)	35
Molly Whyte (10)	35
Dias Jones (9)	36
Andrew Whittle (7)	36
Lauren Miller (10)	37
Jasmine Sparrow (11)	37
Daniel Lowbridge (7)	37
Cassie Burch (11)	38
Harry Almey (10)	38
Ryan Robinson (10)	39
Ellie Whyte (11)	39
Chelsey Ashburner (11)	40
Micha Marie Oates (9)	40
Claire Larkin (11)	41
Laura Houston (11)	41
Stephen Darroch (8)	41
Hugo Tansley (11)	42
James Holland (11)	42
Emma Harvey (11)	43
Charlotte Maxted (11)	43
Ryan Kershaw (10)	44
Chris Maflin (11)	44
Tony Parkes (11)	45
Robert Willway (9)	45
William Robinson (9)	46
Daniel Nordqvist (10)	46
Jack Emberson (10)	46

Carlton Hill Primary School, East Sussex

Christchurch CE School, St Leonards On Sea

Firle CE Primary School, Lewes

Noah Marsh (8)	60
Lisken Jellings (9)	61
Sophia Blee (9)	62
Edith Burns (9)	62
Matthew Ashton Tye (9)	63
Zannia Kidd (8)	63
Ryan Peirce (8)	63
Ben Morris (9)	64

Heron Way Primary School, Horsham

Zac Burchell (11)	64
Lara Cardew (11)	65
Nicola Carter (11)	65
Jenifer Bloomfield (11)	66
Emma Brown (11)	67
Laura Brooke-Simmons (11)	67
Nick Freeman (11)	68
Phoebe Douthwaite-Hodges (11)	68
Natassja Etherington (11)	69
Catherine Bevan (11)	69
Jonathan Knapman (10)	70
Robert Potter (11)	71
Glenn Hunter (11)	71
Tessa Smith (11)	72
Oscar Smith (11)	72
Jack Stocker (10)	73
Samantha Thornton-Rice (11)	73
Anna Wilson (11)	74
Mark McKinney (11)	74
Alice Stennett (11)	75

Hoddern Junior School, Peacehaven

Emily Grimble (9)	75
Bethany Donegan (8)	75
Annie Brooks (9)	76
Saffron Amis (8)	76
Grace Tobin (9)	77
Laura Day (9)	77
Shelby Teale (9)	78

Pebsham CP School, Bexley-on-Sea

Rhianna Light (8)	78
Kirsty Hoggins (11)	79
Hannah Rancic (10)	79
Adam Hollands (10)	80
Billy Reeves (10)	80
Jordan Byford (9)	80
Hazel Holland (11)	81
Cassandra Kourti (8)	81
Mustafa Hamed (11)	81
Elle Lakin (9)	82
Joshua Page (8)	82
Zoe Henderson (11)	83
Ben Watts (11)	84
Jordan Gildersleeve (10)	84
Marcus Winchester (10)	85
Samuel Russell (9)	85
Michelle Wadey (11)	85
James Clark (10)	86
Holly Gearing (11)	86
Kayleigh Louise Dann (10)	87
Jamie Cowling (10)	87
Shannon Beeching (9)	87
Leanne Colvin (11)	88
Georgia Martin (10)	88
April Grant (11)	89
Ryan Morgan (11)	89
Amber Marie Hayler (11)	90
Sam Walters (11)	90
Keeley Pavlis (8)	91

St Leonards CE Primary School, St Leonards-on-Sea

Martyn Durrant (11)	91
Kelly Fairall (11)	92
Brook Tate (10)	92
Joel Phillips (11)	92
Jack Torode (11)	93
Lily Bostanabad (10)	93
Katie Kirkby (11)	94
Emma Rose (11)	94
Daniella Ratnarajah (10)	95

Ryan Couchman (11)	95
Lauren Fuller (11)	96
Georgina Parlour (11)	96
Ivan Miller (11)	97
Shani White (11)	97
Matthew Viney (10)	98
Austin Delamaine (11)	98
Kirsty Alice Sinden (10)	99
Hannah Crouch (10)	99

St Mark's CE School, Brighton

Kayleigh Thurmer (11)	99
Esme Cole (9)	100
Emma Holdway (9)	101
Kayleigh Rosario (9)	102
Chloe Openshaw (8)	103
Charlotte Rolf (9)	104
Zoe Fortune (8)	105
Reece Taylor	105
Calum Adams (9)	106
Liam Terry (9)	106
Nicole Waites (9)	107
Lacey Cole (9)	108
Bethany Dahr (9)	109
Peter Henderson (9)	110
Anab Dahir (10)	110
Lily Mateer (9)	111
Tia Riddle (11)	111
Joanne Short (11)	112
Jay Gander (11)	112
Alex Deacon (11)	112
Nina Sarfas (11)	113
Sophie Joyce (11)	113
Connor Mateer (11)	113
Jamie Palmer	114
Danielle Anderson (11)	114
Esme Sarfas (11)	115
Jessica Wilson	115
Nicola Rosario (11)	116

Telscombe Cliffs CP School, Peacehaven

Georgia Smith (10)	116
Olivia Fisher (9)	116
Emma Brown (9)	117
Rebecca Mason (9)	117
Hayley Clothier (9)	117
Hannah Tolley (8)	118
Luke Harding (8)	118
Ria French (7)	119
Charlotte Stuart (8)	119
Libby Rose Luffingham (8)	120
Bethany Highsted (9)	121
Faye Jones (9)	122
Gabriella Siân Weston (9)	122
Jessica Spice (9)	122
Sharna Elise Vine (9)	123
Daniel Tribe (8)	123
Vanessa Tait (8)	124
Connor Gaul (8)	124
Mark Lee-Falcon (9)	125
Abigail Stuart (10)	125
Natasha Gravett (7)	126
Emilyn Louise Hulatt (10)	126
Kevin Gunn (8)	127
Bethany Yeates (9)	127
Connor McGill (9)	128
Rhys Wheeler (10)	128
Sasha West (9)	129
Kim Bowles (9)	129
Luke Ashdown (8)	130
Nataly Spice (9)	130
Georgia Budd (9)	131
Rafe Hall (8)	131
Lianne Sullivan & Zoe Willard (8)	132
Charly Letts (10)	132
Harry Wallace (9)	133
Hayley Greenfield (9)	133
Dylan Brooks (7)	133
Caiah Morash (9)	134
Eve Plumridge (9)	135
Harry Norman & Adam Leadbitter (9)	136

Victoria Collings (10)	157
Ashley Mark Derrick (9)	157
Kristy Lewis (10)	158
Jamie Gardner (9)	158
Rebecca Seabrook & Megan Horscraft (11)	159
Kelsey Welch (10)	159
Liam Hannigan (10)	160

West Blatchington Junior School, Hove

Michelle Hills (8)	160
Sam McCormick (9)	161
Ben McCormick (8)	161
Rebekah Elphick (10)	162
Shannon Brown (10)	162
Stephanie Batts (7)	163
Rahima Begum (10)	163
Lucy Bone (9)	164
Ayesha Begum (9)	164
Kimberley Holdaway (8)	165
Lee Rebbeck (7)	165
Sara Gurcuoglu (9)	166
Hayley Greco (9)	166
Syd Wilson (8)	167
Sandra Sidarous (8)	167
Adam Mates (8)	168
Emma Perry (8)	168

The Poems

Nature's Numbers

One obeying ostrich
Two tickly tigers
Three thrilling thrushes
Four freaky frogs
Five fantastic fishes
Six snowboarding snakes
Seven snorting seals
Eight excited eagles
Nine nibbling nightingales
Ten tracing tarantulas.

Matt Morrish (7)
Balfour Junior School, Brighton

Mildred Hubble

Mildred Hubble
Lots of trouble
Likes to fly
In a muddle
She loves her tabby
Who makes her happy
Her best friend's Maud
Who never gets bored.

Betsy Robertson (8)
Balfour Junior School, Brighton

Bill Gates Is So Important

I am Bill Gates
I am so cool
I made Microsoft
And that's pretty cool
It made me rich
So remember it all
I am more important than you all.

Jack Burns (8)
Balfour Junior School, Brighton

Nature's Numbers

One obedient ostrich
Two tubby tigers
Three thrilled thrushes
Four familiar flamingos
Five famous frogs
Six slimy snails
Seven secret seagulls
Eight excited eagles
Nine nasty nits
Ten terrifying terrapins.

Connor Bailey (8)
Balfour Junior School, Brighton

Nature's Numbers

One old ostrich
Two tall tortoises
Three thirsty thrushes
Four fast ferrets
Five fierce foxes
Six small swans
Seven scary snakes
Eight enormous eagles
Nine nice nightingales
Ten terrible terrapins.

James Leckey (8)
Balfour Junior School, Brighton

Pop Star

I'm a pop star, I sing all night
My big leather boots shine in the moonlight
I have a cat called Kitty
And sometimes she is awful witty
The fans cheer and clap as my feet tap!

Alexandra Ward (8)
Balfour Junior School, Brighton

Frog And Toad

There was once a frog
Who lived in a bog
And a toad
Who lived by the road

The toad was alone
The frog had a bone
The toad wanted the bone
The frog wanted to be alone

He gave the bone
The toad wasn't alone
The frog was alone
Without a home.

Anand Bhakta (8)
Balfour Junior School, Brighton

There Was A Young Mole

There was a young mole
That had lived down a hole
He lived next to the river
So he would always quiver
He jumped in the water
Swam just a quarter
And then sank the rest of the way!

Luke Bailey (8)
Balfour Junior School, Brighton

What's In My Room?

Mountains of mess
Numerous piles of chocolate wrappers
One weird outfit
Probably a podgy panda.

Emily Newell & Rosie Bates (8)
Balfour Junior School, Brighton

Greedy Pig

There once was a greedy pig called Fatty
He was also once selfish and thought to be batty
He was pink and hairy, short and stout
But when he was angry he couldn't half shout.

There was also a monkey selling food
It was a bright blue day and he was in a good mood
The pig was hungry he smelled the feast
His big pink snout started leading him east.

He scampered on following the trail
Until he saw the monkey's long brown tail
He shoved the monkey and taking the grub
He walked away to eat at the pub.

He walked along pushing the load
Singing a song on a cobble stone road
There was a small animal that asked for a share
Fatty said no and roared like a bear.

He took it to the Savannah to eat on his own
No one could find him even by phone
He scoffed it all, every last bit
And started feeling very sick.

He decided to go home and have a nice rest
But he couldn't move even though he tried his best
The monkey saw him and had an idea
The pig was watching and got filled up with fear.

Monkey went to lion who was big, fat and scary
The animal went and told him about pig on the prairie
The lion agreed in his sort of way
They walked across the desert for the rest of the day.

As soon as the lion saw the pig he jumped up and gave a roar
The pig squealed and screamed until he was no more
The monkey and the lion were friends and that's the end of the story
I hope this poem wins a prize even if it's gory.

Joseph Doherty (8)
Balfour Junior School, Brighton

Animal Fun

One orange octopus offering oats
Two talking tigers tottering through tiles
Three thinking thrushes thinking thoughtfully
Four flipping frogs flipping frantically
Five fearsome fish frightening foxes
Six silly salmon smelling sandwiches
Seven sorry swifts serving sausages
Eight eating elephants eat everything
Nine naughty gnats nicking nails
Ten tired turtles tickling tongues

Lewis Jacobs (8)
Balfour Junior School, Brighton

Poor Patty

Poor Patty pours porridge
Poor Polly practices piano privately, Polly's pretty
Patty's picking prickly pinecones
Patty pricks Polly's poodle
Poor Polly's poodle
Pink poodle paddles purple puddles
Perished Patty perished poor Patty's poodle
Poor Patty!

Georgia Borenius (8)
Balfour Junior School, Brighton

The Railway Track

An orange sat on the railway track
It's breath was filled with butter
Along came a train the 9.30
Toot! Toot! Orange splatter!

Nathan Luke De Freitas (7)
Balfour Junior School, Brighton

Crazy Poem

One odd owl
Two terrifying tortoises
Three tiny tigers
Four frightened fish
Five funny friends
Six scary snakes
Seven slimy snails
Eight evil elephants
Nine nosy nuts
Ten tangled tents
Eleven excellent eggs
Twelve tweeting TVs.

Celine Antal (8)
Balfour Junior School, Brighton

One Obedient Octopus

One obedient octopus
Two talented turtles
Three thoughtful tigers
Four finding fish
Five fat frogs
Six slithering slugs
Seven slithering snakes
Eight Egyptian eels.

Reuben Bowers (7)
Balfour Junior School, Brighton

Camel

A camel sat on the railway track
The only one in Dover
He tried to escape the 9.15
Too late he got ran over!

Bethan Davies (7)
Balfour Junior School, Brighton

Animals Breakout

One opaque otter offering oranges
Two tired turtles tallying terrapins
Three threatening tigers terrifying tabbies
Four fierce florists frightening fiddlers
Five fiery fireflies fluttering fragile
Six slinky squirrels slipping smoothly
Seven strange slugs sliding slowly
Eight evil Easter eggs eating everything
Nine nasty nickels nibbling newts
Ten terrible toes tragically tiptoeing.

Holly Clarke (8)
Balfour Junior School, Brighton

Don't Tell

Don' t tell I kicked my brother's ball
Don't tell it went over the wall
I really ripped my teacher's book
When she was not there and couldn't look
I nearly tripped up my dad
When that happened I was very sad
I secretly climbed up a tree
When I was up there I was stung by a bee
I was told to take down the flag
When I did I looked in your bag.

Gary Moscovici (8)
Balfour Junior School, Brighton

Animals In The World

One opaque owl offering old octopuses
Two tall tortoises tumbling to trains
Three thin thrushes throwing thorns
Four fat fish flying for fitness
Five fit frogs fishing for fish.

Finlay White (7)
Balfour Junior School, Brighton

Millie's Pets

Millie had some squeaking pets
So she had to take them to the vet
One of them ran away
Millie thought she would come back

Then I met a friend called Billy
And hasn't been found till this day
The pets were really mad
Millie was sad
One day the pets set off
Then they met the pet on the computer
Then they lived happily ever after.

Isabelle Clacher (8)
Balfour Junior School, Brighton

Lucy

A girl called Lucy she has a pet tiger
She lived in a white house with a spider
One day they had a walk
The tiger took some pork
They bumped into a dark hood
And Lucy thought they were in a wood
When they went back home Lucy opened the window.

Martha Southon (7)
Balfour Junior School, Brighton

Alliteration

One occupied otter offering oranges
Two tamed tortoises tallying trees
Three thrashed thrushes thundering through them
Four friendly frogs freaking out
Five fiery fish frightening frogs
Six slippery snakes shout, 'Shoooo!'

Lewis George (8)
Balfour Junior School, Brighton

I'm Already In Trouble Today

I'm already in trouble today
I don't need any more
I'm not allowed out to play
For throwing an apple core

I didn't mean to hit Miss Syms
I was aiming at the bins
I'm already in trouble today
I don't need any more

So now I'm sitting good as gold
Even though it's really cold
I didn't mean to kick the ball
And make a hole in the wall

Oh look she's coming up to me
I really hope she didn't see

Yes, all right I'll be good forever more!

Ellen Hayward-Butcher (8)
Balfour Junior School, Brighton

How Animals Act!

One orange octopus
Two twin turtles
Three thousand thorns
Four friendly fishes
Five freezing foxes
Six slimy snakes
Seven silly snails
Eight eager eagles
Nine nice newts
Ten thoughtful teddies.

Ella Turvil (7)
Balfour Junior School, Brighton

Tomato Ketchup

A tomato sat on a road
Just like a little toad
He went 'eek!' the car went 'beep! beep!'
It was an Aston Martin who did it
Now it is tomato ketchup!

Charlie Patch (8)
Balfour Junior School, Brighton

A Snake Sat Slithering Along The Railway Track

A snake sat slithering along the railway track
Along came a train the 9.15
The snake's heart was really scared
The snake slithered home.

George Miller (7)
Balfour Junior School, Brighton

A Bunny Sat On The Railway Track

A bunny sat on the railway track
It's heart was all a groan
Along came a train at 10.51
Toot! Toot! It hopped home.

Elliot Godden (8)
Balfour Junior School, Brighton

The Boy And The Granny

There once was a boy who lived in a grey house
He knocked on an old granny's door
A monster came out, 'Aaaarrrggghhh!'
He ate the boy up!

Jonathan Sang (8)
Balfour Junior School, Brighton

One Odd Otter

One odd otter
Two tidy twins
Three tall trees
Four flipping fish
Five flying frogs
Six scary snakes
Seven slow surfers
Eight eager eels
Nine nice newts
Ten terrifying tigers.

Athol Ruston (7)
Balfour Junior School, Brighton

Tuna

A tuna fish swam in a harbour
His heart was a clutter
Along came a ship
The Sea Angel, I think
Honk! Honk!
Tuna's for dinner.

Eddie Clarke (8)
Balfour Junior School, Brighton

Strange Animals

One odd octopus
Two twin turtles
Three terrible tigers
Four fine fish
Five flirting foxes
Six slithering snakes.

Isabella Tyndall Bristow (7)
Balfour Junior School, Brighton

Mad Animals

One ogre octopus
Two typhoon turtles
Three thirsty tigers
Four fantastic foxes
Five funky fish
Six silly snakes
Seven surfing surfers
Eight exclusive elephants
Nine nursing ninjas
Ten turning tigers.

Ella Pennington Brightwell (7)
Balfour Junior School, Brighton

Numbered Animals

One old owl
Two tangled tigers
Three tiny tillies
Four fancy flamingos
Five flirting fish
Six sour salmon
Seven slithering snakes
Eight English elephants.

Elena Ward (7)
Balfour Junior School, Brighton

An Apple Sat On The Railway Track

An apple sat on the railway track
Its brain was all of a-flutter
Along came a train the 9.16
Toot! Toot! *Aaaarrrggghhh!*
Sploosh! Apple juice!

Dylan Reah (8)
Balfour Junior School, Brighton

The King And Queen

One day there was a king and queen
Who lived in a castle called Spooky Baby
They went in a carriage to a ball
The queen had two babies called Gail and Amber
They all went to the ball and danced
They lived happily ever after.

Chelsea Young (8)
Balfour Junior School, Brighton

Rugby Spirit

Rugby is a physical game
It isn't played for the money or fame
Jonny Wilkinson kicks the goals
And the Australians shout loud
The team drinks Lucozade
But everyone else likes lemonade
Everyone says it's rough
And you have to be tough.

Joshua Kemp (11)
Barnham Primary School, Barnham

You Shine Like The Sun

You shine like the sun bright and beautiful
You shine like the sun lovely and nice
The colours on you are yellow and orange
So bright and nice
You are so wonderful
You shine like the sun, you are so warm
You shine like the sun you feel so lovely.

Jessica Spain (8)
Barnham Primary School, Barnham

Creepy Woman In My House

I woke up sleepy
I heard something creepy
I came out my room
And tripped over a broom
I went down the stairs
With all my cares
I stopped and opened the door

There, looking at me
Was something black and scary
Am I asleep
Or am I a creep?
Now! This thing black
Looks like a Mac
And held something shiny

I turn on the light
I jumped back with fright
When it was only my mum
She stuck up her thumb.

Georgina Denyer (10)
Barnham Primary School, Barnham

Conversation

'I'm going to the shops'
'Why?'
'Because I'm getting food'
'Why?'
'Because I'm hungry'
'Why?'
'Stop saying why'
'Why?'
'Because I'll chop your head off'
'So'
'You'll be dead . . .'

Jed Bates (8)
Barnham Primary School, Barnham

My Family

My gran likes tea
And loses her key
But she just loves me

I have a brother
And two others
Sometimes they're so bad
They drive me mad

My mum cleans for hours
She likes her colourful flowers
She likes her bed
And she kisses me on the head

My dad is so cool
He has some rules
But sometimes he acts
Like the family fool

My grandad has no hair
He is as big as a bear
He is fair
He always cares

My nan is so sweet
Like a little treat
She is a lady
You would want to meet.

Megan Mead (10)
Barnham Primary School, Barnham

Sunshine Haiku

There in the sunshine
You were so bright yesterday
Like a burning ball.

Holly Dean (7)
Barnham Primary School, Barnham

The Lady On The Sun

The lady on the sun
Has a great amount of fun
While sitting there sucking her thumb

She's a little old lady
With a two-year-old baby
And the baby says to her mum, 'Maybe'

The little lady sometimes gets burnt
The first time she did it she learnt

For learning she thought she earned a present
So her two-year-old baby brought her a present
And the pheasant came from a garden crescent.

Rosie Beller (10)
Barnham Primary School, Barnham

Children's Prayer

Let the teachers obey our rules
Forget about tests and trash all the schools!
Let us eat whatever we wish
We want pizza not fish!
I wish teachers were never here
I don't even want them near
I wish the teachers were little mice
So I can eat them with lots of rice.

Charlotte Tester (9)
Barnham Primary School, Barnham

The Sea

I went in the sea a great way out
I know I will drown without a doubt
I thought I saw some floating bark
No it's not! It's a great white shark!

Ben Root (8)
Barnham Primary School, Barnham

The Seasons

Springtime is such fun
It brings joy to everyone
The new life is here
Summer brings great fun
Hot sunshine and swimming fun!
Fruit becomes ripe, yum!
Leaves are falling down
Leaves are swirling round and round
Falling to the ground
It snows in winter
Snowmen stiff in the snow
Children throw snowballs.

**Declan, Micha Oates, Emily, Charlotte Tester,
Dannia, Scot & Jack Spear**
Barnham Primary School, Barnham

Epitaph For Mr Mystery

There was a teacher called Mr Mystery
Whose favourite subject was history
His favourite pupil was Tom
Then he got killed by a bomb!

William Green (9)
Barnham Primary School, Barnham

Dog Haiku

Why are you fluffy?
Why do you have a long tail?
You are so cuddly!

Emily Rudge (9)
Barnham Primary School, Barnham

Ryan

Small boy
Tonka toy
Stinky toes
Big fat nose
Watch TV
Love CBBC
Big brother
Love each other
Hates roast
Loves toast
Gelled up hair
Loves his teddy bear
Horrible habits
Kicks his rabbit
That's what makes Ryan, Ryan.

Matthew Kerr (10)
Barnham Primary School, Barnham

Playing In The Snow

Snow fight
All white
Snowflake
Arm break
All cold
Gloves sold
Now it's freezing
I am sneezing
Mum said I've got a cold
But my snowman is getting old.

Jessie Laker (8)
Barnham Primary School, Barnham

Giant

Hair like yellow string
Head like a big yellow ball
Eyes like massive clocks
Nose like a long branch
Mouth like a piece of a water melon
Lips like squashed raspberries
Voice like giant
Breath like rotten bananas
Teeth like pointed pencils
Ears like black craggy cauliflowers
Neck like a giraffe
Body like a big mountain
Heart like burnt ash
Arms like long rulers
Hands like hairy gorillas
Legs like long poles
Feet like floppy jelly
Toes like melting chocolate.

Freya Holland (8)
Barnham Primary School, Barnham

Conversation

'I'm going to the park'
'Why?'
'Because I want to go to the park'
'Why?'
'To play football'
'Why?'
'To score goals'
'Why?'
'Why do you keep on saying why?'
'What?'

Jamie West (9)
Barnham Primary School, Barnham

Conversation

'I'm going to get an ice cream'
'Why?'
'Because it's hot'
'Why?'
'Because it's summer'
'Why?'
'It's sunny'
'Why?'
'Because I'm almost on fire'
'Why?'
'Will you stop saying why?'
'Why?'

Aaron Green (9)
Barnham Primary School, Barnham

Bike Riding

Bike riding
Never hiding

Feel the breeze
In the trees

Dodge the log
Mind the dog

See the tree
Oh there's a bee.

James Stephenson (8)
Barnham Primary School, Barnham

Epitaph For Mike

Here lies a teacher called Mike
He got hit by a bike
He's in heaven
Sitting with Kevin.

Zac Rigby (9)
Barnham Primary School, Barnham

Conversation

'I'm going to get a drink of lemonade'
'Why?'
'Because I'm hot'
'Why?'
'Because it's sunny'
'Why?'
'Because it's summer'
'It's time for you to stop saying why'
'Oohhhhh . . .'

Logan Sword (9)
Barnham Primary School, Barnham

Fire, Burn And Cauldron Bubble

Round and round the water goes
So I can eat your bones
You mix it with a dog's tongue
I'll put in a boy who is young
Stir, stir, stir the pot
Make sure it will never stop
Newt's eye
And say goodbye
Before I go to bed
I will eat your head.

George Bathews (9)
Barnham Primary School, Barnham

Epitaph

Here lies the body of Miss Steenhoff
She jumped off a cliff and was never seen of
Where did she escape they say?
Maybe we will see her another day?

Nathan Green (8)
Barnham Primary School, Barnham

Thin Poem

House mouse
Big cat
Smack cat
Got fat
Cat hat
Sat mat
More lice
That's nice.

Dominic Sibun (8)
Barnham Primary School, Barnham

Mrs Porter

Here lies the body of Mrs Porter
Unfortunately she was afraid of water
On the bottom of the pool she hit her head
Now the cowardly women's dead.

Robert Edward Walker (8)
Barnham Primary School, Barnham

Prayer

Protect me from the dragon under the stairs
Protect me from the grizzly bears.

Callum Boxall (8)
Barnham Primary School, Barnham

Summer Haiku

Why are you so hot?
Because I am sunbathing
In a sunny pot.

Kieran Hornsby (8)
Barnham Primary School, Barnham

Conversation

'I am going to the shop'
'Why?'
'To get some clothes'
'Why?'
'Because I am going to a party tommorow'
'Why?'
'Because my old clothes have got holes in'
'Why'
'Because I have worn them out'
'Why?'
'What does why mean?'
'What?'

Emily Golding (8)
Barnham Primary School, Barnham

Children's Prayer

I wish the teachers gave us tests
So they say we are the best
I wish the teachers gave us sweets
And gave us little goody treats
Let us eat what we please
But don't give me butter and cheese
I wish the children ruled the school
So all the boys can play football.

Blake Brundle (9)
Barnham Primary School, Barnham

Epitaph

There was a teacher called Mr Codd
Who was shot down by PC Podd
His real name was Paul
He worked at a school.

Ryan Burch (9)
Barnham Primary School, Barnham

Children's Prayer

I wish golden time was always ticked
I wish the teachers were never strict
I wish we could have lots of sweets
Coke and ice cream they are our treats
I wish we can go out all the time
Because that is not really a crime
I wish the teachers do obey
All the things we always say.

Hannah Ide (9)
Barnham Primary School, Barnham

A Bird's Daily Thing

Flying over towns
Flying over hills
Flying over seas
Swooping down below
Pecking on the ground
Getting worms to eat
It's a bird's daily thing.

Millie Hobbs (10)
Barnham Primary School, Barnham

Wind

When I am alone
I listen to the wind whistle
Slowly, slowly
It fades away
I feel alone again.

Samantha-Anne Glover (9)
Barnham Primary School, Barnham

The Young Boy

There was a young boy in school
That always jumped in the pool
He would dive and he would jump
While they were still using the pump
And he really thought he was cool.

Gavin Kerr (8)
Barnham Primary School, Barnham

The Sea

I went out to sea
But oh my what did I see?
A whale leaping into the air!
He was bigger than the boat and that was the end
Of the whale that looped into the air.

Luke Elsworth (9)
Barnham Primary School, Barnham

When I Am Alone

When I am alone
I hear the cold wind below
I like the peaceful snow
It's like it is glowing
Snow hits my feet.

Thomas Paget (9)
Barnham Primary School, Barnham

Epitaph For Mr Jones

Here lies Mr Jones
He's just a bag of bones
He didn't get far
Because he got hit by a car and will never be seen again.

Declan Pawsey (9)
Barnham Primary School, Barnham

Where Is That Teacher?

Where is the teacher that helped me with my tests?
Where is the teacher that helped me with my pests?
Where is the teacher that stopped me biting?
Where is the teacher that stopped me fighting?
Where is the teacher that shouts at me
Because I was playing with my bike key?
Where is the teacher that said that I am good
'Cause I always tried?

Callum Brundle (11)
Barnham Primary School, Barnham

How Do I Love Them?

How do I love thee? I would die for you
Do you think you could die for me too?
I would never let you go, I need you by my side
If I ever lost you, I would hunt for you far and wide

Whenever I see you, you brighten up my day
'I love you,' that's what I say.

Danni J Noble (9)
Barnham Primary School, Barnham

How Do I Love Thee?

How do I love thee? If I lost you my life
Would not be worth living
I love you to death and I would never let you go
How do I love thee? If I lost you
My heart would be broken and it would
Take my breath away.

Charlotte Edwards (9)
Barnham Primary School, Barnham

I've Always Wanted . . .

I have always wanted to meet an alien
I've heard that they're quite rare
I've always wanted to explore the galaxy
I've always wanted to be a spaceman
I've always wanted to work on satellites
I've always wanted to send messages back to Earth
I've always wanted to be a veteran pilot
I've always wanted to be the admiral of Starfleet
I've always wanted to invade other planets
I've always wanted to capture aliens
I've always wanted to crush red aliens
I've always wanted to be a space marine
I've always wanted to work with explosives
I've always wanted to wear armour
I've always wanted to shoot lasers.

Rory Myers (11)
Barnham Primary School, Barnham

Coloured Snooker Balls

Red, I leave early to go on my pooey moped
Yellow, when I get there the girly girls say hello
Green, I try to hide but I am always seen
Brown, they say that they wear a crown
Blue, I hate them they smell of poo
Pink, I'm not joking they really do stink
Black, they play football I bet they hack
White, I wish I could push them from a great height
Snooker, sometimes I want to blow them up with a bazooka.

Craig Dummer (11)
Barnham Primary School, Barnham

The Race

One won
Two went blue
Three ate a pea
Four was galore
And five was alive

Six was a fix
Seven went to Devon
Eight was very late
Nine was fine
And ten met a hen

Eleven was in heaven
Twelve met Clelve
Thirteen was still clean
Fourteen was mean
And fifteen went green

Sixteen had a machine
Seventeen was lean
Eighteen hurt his spleen
Nineteen wasn't seen
And twenty now had plenty.

Holly Challinor (10)
Barnham Primary School, Barnham

My Prayer

Protect me from witches
Protect me from bears
Protect me from the dragon under the stairs.

Shannon Parrott (8)
Barnham Primary School, Barnham

Best Mates

Me and my friend
Oh how we spend and lend
We're the same size
We never tell lies
We fit each other's clothes
Old and new
We sunbathe together
We're friends together
We're on the phone 24/7
Just in case we turn 11
We're in the same year
And wear the same gear
Our eyes the same, like a pair of shoes
Blue and green to make them seen
We have the same taste
That I'll never, never waste

We're best mates together
Forever always.

Megan Collier (10)
Barnham Primary School, Barnham

Me And My Mate

Me and my mate
We stay out late
We go out to shops
Have so much fun
We go see scary movies
But never get scared
We will never break up
Because we're best mates.

Chelsea Betsworth (10)
Barnham Primary School, Barnham

Today I Ate . . .

Today I ate . . .
2 chocolate cakes
5 strawberry biscuits
2 hamburgers
3 cheese sandwiches
1 mint cornetto
4 apples
2 bottles of orange
And a carrot

At eight o'clock I went to bed
At eighty-thirty I puked
I puked up . . .
A carrot
2 bottles of orange
4 apples
1 mint cornetto
3 cheese sandwiches
2 hamburgers
5 strawberry biscuits
And 2 chocolate cakes

Tomorrow I will
Have a breath

The day after
Tomorrow
I may have
A bottle of orange
But not at this moment
Thanks.

Grace Pidgeon (9)
Barnham Primary School, Barnham

Litter

In the busy city street above London's bustling feet
Litter rots and litter lies
Killing animals in the skies

Cars and petrol taking up the streets
These streets are far from neat, above
London's bustling feet

On the beach it's even worse
The sea's polluted with oil and dirt
Causing pain and mess and hurt

When will this world see the light?
All this pollution's just not right
What an awful, awful sight
To see in this city every night
Will we ever win the fight?

Bradley Cranwell (11)
Barnham Primary School, Barnham

My Friends

My friend Katie
Walks like she's eighty
Whenever she sees her mates

My friend Daniel
Walks at an angle
But always has to strangle

My friend Molly
Always licks lollies
Whenever she's playing with Mollie

My friend Sam
Sat by the dam
Watching the fish as they swam.

Louise Chapman (10)
Barnham Primary School, Barnham

Today I Ate . . .

Today I ate . . .
3 pieces of chocolate cake
A fanta
2 cheeseburgers
4 chocolate cornettos
5 peanut butter sandwiches
And a peach

At 7.30pm I went to bed
At 8.00pm I threw up

The day after tomorrow I might eat . . .
A fanta
1 cornetto
1 cheeseburger
And 1 peanut butter sandwich.

Abbie Smith (10)
Barnham Primary School, Barnham

A Mystery Creature

A beautiful face
A pace like grace

A gorgeous mane
Which dances in the rain

Three white socks
That clip and clop

It bucks and rears
Like the three musketeers

Can you guess what she is?
. . . A horse.

Charlotte Dean (10)
Barnham Primary School, Barnham

Vampire

If you go out on your own
A vampire stalks you
He'll crush your bones
Take your brain
And then make you into a stew

Vampire vampire why did you do that?
I saw every little bit
You'll be very fat
Just like a cow
If you keep on doing it

I'm sorry Jim it's a habit
I can't just do nothing
Maybe I can become fat
No I can't
Because then you'll keep on laughing

It worked out fine
And I'm not joking
But I'm still sticking to blood wine.

Mazharul Islam (11)
Barnham Primary School, Barnham

Mr Elephant

Mr Elephant big and grey
I saw Mr Elephant eating hay
Mr Elephant's ears are like fans
So he ate his way through cans
Mr Elephant's trunk's like a hose
And he's always ready to pose
Mr Elephant has lots of friends
And they all have different trends.

Billy Court (10)
Barnham Primary School, Barnham

Crazy Castle Journey

There was a boy called Tony Parcel
On his way to Crazy Castle
To deliver a present to the owner
Called Professor Super Lobber Bowler

On the road of slim and stare
Came the breed of Night-Mare
With a horse and young Tony's gift
Wasn't to be seen by dustbin ponies

Along the way the two saw a troll
Who said, 'Are you two having a stroll
To Crazy Castle? I'll come too!'
And into the forest they went through

Then there was a skeleton, sad and grumpy
The three would have him, if he wasn't so lumpy
The bony guy followed them, until they saw
Crazy Castle's open door

They all stepped inside to have a small peep
Although the four got pummelled by a broom sweep
Then they all fell on top of an old dusty mat
But it was a trap and they went . . . *splat!*

Professor Bowler had set this all up
And celebrated by drinking from a small cup
Everyone forgot about Tony Parcel
For he should never have gone to Crazy Castle.

Toby Parry (11)
Barnham Primary School, Barnham

Crocodile Haiku

The crocodile snaps
He slips into the water
He might eat you up!

Nathan Hall (7)
Barnham Primary School, Barnham

My School

My school is the best
It beats all the rest
If you swing on your chair
The teacher becomes a grizzly bear

Our teachers are so tall
They are still so cool
We listen to what she has to say
Until the end of the day

The school is all blue
We do our work, yes we do
We work really well
As you can simply tell

The class all giggle
We can't sit still we wriggle
But if you can see
Our school will always be
The best school in the world.

Kjersti Napier-Raikes (11)
Barnham Primary School, Barnham

Bird's-Eye View

Over the hills, under the clouds
Through the trees and under the bridges
An amazing view you will find

The hills are massive mounds of mint
Ice cream in a cone of land and sea

The lakes are melted sapphires
Homing hundreds of fish

The trees are lime flavoured lollipops
Protruding from the middle of the Earth

The birds fly over everything
Loving the bird's eye view.

Molly Whyte (10)
Barnham Primary School, Barnham

Horse

Horse
Enormous
Mighty
Bitey
White
Black
Tail
Fast
Jumping
Carrying
Racing
Smart.

Dias Jones (9)
Barnham Primary School, Barnham

Rat

Rat
Splat
Grey
White
Tail
Active
Crawl
Wall
Corn
Down
Eat
Sweet.

Andrew Whittle (7)
Barnham Primary School, Barnham

An Elephant

A large eater
A scaly thing
A slow mover
A grey creature
A heavy lump
A hairy beast
A strong fighter
A plant eater
A mud roller
An elephant.

Lauren Miller (10)
Barnham Primary School, Barnham

A People Hunter

A people hunter
A sly swimmer
A sharp thinker
A blood smeller
A meat eater
A swift killer
A shark.

Jasmine Sparrow (11)
Barnham Primary School, Barnham

Dogs Haiku

Dogs are very fast
Dogs are very loveable
Dogs are very smart.

Daniel Lowbridge (7)
Barnham Primary School, Barnham

Zoo Haikus

Lions
Prowling, pouncing, fierce
Searching, hunting for it's prey
Never to be seen

Parrot
Loud ear piercing squawk
Chattering to passers-by
Then flies away home

Elephant
A loud trumpet noise
Spraying water from it's hose
Trudging round all day

Giraffe
Spots like chicken pox
It's long neck's like a ladder
Stretching to the leaves

Zebra
It chomps the green grass
People cross it's striped body
While it sleeps all night.

Cassie Burch (11)
Barnham Primary School, Barnham

Mr Cheetah

Mr Cheetah as quick as lightning
Mr Cheetah is good at fighting
Mr Cheetah has eyes like jewels
Mr Cheetah in a sprint never stalls

Mr Cheetah has very good eyes
Mr Cheetah uses them as spies
Mr Cheetah eats his prey
Mr Cheetah runs away.

Harry Almey (10)
Barnham Primary School, Barnham

My Family

My dad is the best
He beats all the rest
He picks his nose
And everyone knows

My brother is so cool
He is actually a fool
I ran him over with a clover
And he couldn't get back up

My mum cooks me dinner
She is such a winner
She will help me tomorrow
And for a year to come

And now you know my family
This poem will finish calmly.

Ryan Robinson (10)
Barnham Primary School, Barnham

Beneath My Feet

Beneath my feet
Beats . . .
The warm water swishes
See the water swish
The silver shells shine
See the shells shine
The sandy seaweed swoshes
See the seaweed swosh
The squirmy starfish swims
See the starfish swim
The sparkling seahorse splashes
See the seahorse splash
Beneath my feet.

Ellie Whyte (11)
Barnham Primary School, Barnham

Gym

I really love gym
How I fling up in the air
And swing back down
I spin and spin in the air
Can't you see
I look like a Catherine wheel
My dear

I really do concentrate
But I chatter so I get told
'Are you the teacher?'
I answer, 'Maybe, can I?'
She sends me out with a temper
I stand alone wishing to go home
At the end she calls my mum
Saying how terrible I've been
While I cry in my head
I only said, 'Stop it!'

Chelsey Ashburner (11)
Barnham Primary School, Barnham

How Do I Love Thee?

How do I love thee?
No need to think
It's all so clear
You are so kind and helpful
You are always near, it brings a tear

You are my intelligent sunshine
You gave me life, you are so nice
You helped me when I was bullied and beaten
You feed me and 'give me a slice'

You're my radiant sunshine, I love you loads
You're so amazing, you are brilliant
You're my radiant sunshine and my wonderful light

Micha Marie Oates (9)
Barnham Primary School, Barnham

Dragon Story

Once upon a time
When stories were told in rhyme
There was a dragon in a cave
And a knight that was very brave

When the knight saw the dragon he was looking lonely
He did a few tricks which made the dragon moany
The dragon told him what was wrong
So the knight played a little song

That made the dragon very sad
And he went home to his dragon dad
The knight said, 'That is such a shame'
They never saw the dragon again.

Claire Larkin (11)
Barnham Primary School, Barnham

My Cat

My cat sleeps all day long
When he sleeps he looks awfully strong
But when he's awake he loves his food
And if he doesn't get it, he's in a mood
When he is in the garden he chews grass
But after, he feels a bit sick
When he goes to the toilet he goes in the flower beds
And comes back smelling
I will always love my cat.

Laura Houston (11)
Barnham Primary School, Barnham

Dragon Of The Wind

Dragon of the wind
Flying through the clouds so swift
Breathing fire like wind.

Stephen Darroch (8)
Barnham Primary School, Barnham

The Lonely Bear

My ripped-up face
My cut up legs
My pulled out eye
Under the bed, with the crunched up wrapper
Of an Easter egg

The loneliness under the bed
Why can't I be played with?
Just because I'm ragged up
There's no reason for me to live

I just want to be popular
That's all I ask
I wouldn't care for anything
I'd just like to have a task.

Hugo Tansley (11)
Barnham Primary School, Barnham

Above The Earth

The sun is a golden yo-yo
Dangling off God's finger
It is a golden bottle top
That has fallen from Heaven

The sky is a huge backdrop
For a play
It is a huge blueprint
Of the Earth

The clouds are huge sponges
Cleaning the watery sky
They are cotton buds
Dabbing the Earth.

James Holland (11)
Barnham Primary School, Barnham

My Best Friends

My friend Billy, acts really silly
Whenever he sees a cat
My friend Mollie, acts like a dolly
Whenever she sees a bat
My friend Betty, sleeps like a yeti
Whenever she feels cold
My friend James, pretends to be flames
Whenever he knows his secret's been told

My friend Todd, swims like a cod
Whenever he sees a shark
My friend Jeb, pretends to be dead
Whenever he's in the dark
My friend Jack eats the footie rack
Whenever he's feeling mad
My friend Clare will always wear
Something that looks really bad.

Emma Harvey (11)
Barnham Primary School, Barnham

What Is This?

A huge floating blob
Aliens' best landing spot
A flying saucer spinning through the galaxy
What is this?
The world.

A giant blue and green smartie
A disco ball from the party
A turner and churner
Still and restless
What is this?
The world.

Charlotte Maxted (11)
Barnham Primary School, Barnham

Sue

If you'd stayed in Manchester this would not have happened, Sue
Now you're in Britain, the no.1 killing city, wasn't that a clue
You said you were going to Arundel, you lied
When I got the phone call, I cried
They said you died
I want to kill the person driving the Ford
I walked along, he said he was bored!
I cannot believe this is the last time I'll see you face to face
In this dark, blood-filled, trashed-up place
The last time I saw you, you were a block of gold
But now you're bronze and extremely cold
Every time I hear your name I get in a fight
That 30 minutes of my life ruined my beautiful sight
Sue.

Ryan Kershaw (10)
Barnham Primary School, Barnham

I Asked A . . .

I asked a chimp, 'What do you drink?'
And in return he said, 'Whisky that's pink'
I wondered what kind of whisky this was
And I thought how much this would cost in dosh
I bought him this, he knew it was from me
So he grabbed my banana and ran up a tree

I asked a croc, 'What do you eat?'
And in return he said, 'Meat'
I assumed he had no more food to spare
So I looked and stood as if I didn't care
But in the end this was not true
And I ended up as that croc's stew.

Chris Maflin (11)
Barnham Primary School, Barnham

Mass Destruction

It sparks a new life
Soon it becomes an army
Mobilising its attacks

It raids the forest
Jolting in different directions
Following the wind's command

It swallows the trees
Leaving only ash
Marching through the wood

It hisses at the birds
Dancing through the bushes
Crackling with laughter

It starts to die
Flicking into darkness
Goes the weapon of mass destruction.

Tony Parkes (11)
Barnham Primary School, Barnham

I See Bobby

I see Bobby lying on the floor
I see Bobby climbing up the door
I see Bobby flying through the air
I see Bobby in his underwear

I see Bobby hiding in the cupboard
I see Bobby playing Old Mother Hubbard
I see Bobby sitting in his bedroom
I see Bobby saying, 'Broom, broom, broom'

I see Bobby sleeping in his bed
I miss Bobby and that's what I said.

Robert Willway (9)
Barnham Primary School, Barnham

Seed

A little seed
A yellow bead

A green stem
A blue gem

A yellow leaf
A sea reef

A pink flower
A lot of power

A diary to make me
Flower.

William Robinson (9)
Barnham Primary School, Barnham

Football

A football is round
It gets kicked around
A football is white
I kick it when it's right
A football is black
I give it a whack
A football.

Daniel Nordqvist (10)
Barnham Primary School, Barnham

Cub

Cub
Kills prey
Rips their flesh
Eats them for tea
Tiger!

Jack Emberson (10)
Barnham Primary School, Barnham

Thunder

It echoes in the valleys
Rounding on the city
Waiting for the call to attack

The sky is still
Nothing's moving
Except the clouds

All of a sudden
The clouds are broken through
By a yellow and white zigzagged line

Like a thousand electric volts
It strikes the ground
Parts of the earth scattered everywhere

A few metres on
Another strike hits a tree
Burning it to a crisp

The thunder gets tired
It moves away, slowly
Leaving the world in pieces.

Jamie Tite (11)
Barnham Primary School, Barnham

Midnight Haikus

Big Ben strikes midnight
The lost child walks on alone
Alone with the stars

Big Ben strikes midday
The loved child walks his way home
Along with his mum.

Alice Etienne (11)
Barnham Primary School, Barnham

What Is . . . The Sky And The Clouds?

It is a . . .
Blue sheet of paper blotted with paint
It is a . . .
Blue light with a cloth over it
It is a . . .
Sea with white fish in it
It is a . . .
Bluebell covered with snow
It is a . . .
Blue cake with white icing
It is a . . .
Blue tiled floor with spilled sugar.

Melissa Gillbard (10)
Barnham Primary School, Barnham

Totally Mental

He walks around with his shoes on his hands
He dances around with fifty rubber bands
He sits at home with his hands on his head
He hugs his jumpers before he goes to bed
He says hello to every tree
He shouts aloud when he sees a bee
He may look gentle
But really he is *totally mental!*

Polly Manners (10)
Barnham Primary School, Barnham

My Name Is Charlotte Preston

My name is Charlotte Preston
I love to scream and shout
I've got two bossy sisters who boss me around
My friend rang me up and I couldn't come out.

Charlotte Preston (11)
Barnham Primary School, Barnham

The Cat

The cat slept silently
While dreaming of pouncing violently on a mouse

His eyes opened wide
As he slipped into the tide and yawned in relief
It was a dream

His ears went up as he heard a call
He ran to his owner being careful not to fall

He leapt into his owners arms
She stroked him and he felt so calm

At last he let out a quiet purr
And let his owner stroke his fur.

Mollie West (10)
Barnham Primary School, Barnham

Doggy

I saw a dog and
It was eating a frog

I told it to go
So it did a puppet show

He saw a rocket and
Got some change out of his pocket

He travelled to the moon with a
Kitchen broom and he was never seen again.

Steven Browne (10)
Barnham Primary School, Barnham

Killer Shark Haiku

Gliding through the sea
Shark's really very angry
He is after me.

Scott Bentley (8)
Barnham Primary School, Barnham

Molly

My best friend Molly
I call her Lolly

She is so kind
She has a great mind

She has brown hair
She really does care

And so that is my best friend!

Stephanie Napier-Raikes (10)
Barnham Primary School, Barnham

A Bad Day Out

I bought a fast car
It got stuck in wet tar
So I went to the zoo
To buy Winnie the Pooh
He left a mess
All over my dress
So I chucked him away
And left in dismay.

Oliver Neill (11)
Barnham Primary School, Barnham

Motorbike, Motorbike

Motorbike, motorbike
Sparkling bright
Motorbike, motorbike
Sitting in the garage
Motorbike, motorbike
Ready to get washed
Motorbike, motorbike
Ready to go.

Dan Lubbe (10)
Barnham Primary School, Barnham

Cats

Big cats, small cats
Fat cats, thin cats
Playful cats, lazy cats
Black cats, white cats
Cuddly cats, bony cats
Scary cats, friendly cats
No tailed freaky cats
Lonely cats, couple cats
Sad cats, happy cats
Tiny little baby cats
They are all the cats I see.

Becky Dickson (10)
Barnham Primary School, Barnham

All In A Day's Work

Get your drink
Get your flowers
Get your food
Get your chips
Get your saucer
Get water
Get filled up
All in a day's work.

Adam Mitchell (10)
Barnham Primary School, Barnham

Matthew

Matthew is my best friend
Our friendship will never end
Even though he's round the bend
My best friend is Matthew Kerr
Even though he does big burps
And hates lemon curd!

Ryan Lee-Smith (10)
Barnham Primary School, Barnham

What's The Colour Of Love?

What's the colour of love?
Is it *blue?* No. It means
It's damp in your heart

Is it *grey?* No. It means
It's cold and raining in your heart
Is it *green?* No. It means
You're smelly and lazy

Is it *red?* Yes. It means
You're happy and joyful.

Ayla Askew (11)
Barnham Primary School, Barnham

Home

Horse run
Course fun
People rides
Huge
Teeth
Fields
Stables
Hays
Poles
Saddle.

Jasmine Welch (8)
Barnham Primary School, Barnham

The Mad Dog

A dog called Tilly
Was very silly
Until he met a man with a hilly
Who took him in
And sold him for a shilling.

Freddie Smithers (10)
Barnham Primary School, Barnham

Little Lizard

Little lizard
Is a wizard
Chasing little flies
He puts them in pastry and turns them into pies
He puts them in his mouth
And heads down south
Going munch, munch, munch
Then crunch, crunch, crunch
When the flies reached his belly
They saw nothing but jelly
Then started buzzing up and down
Looking around
Little lizard felt sick
He went hick, hick, hick
Little lizard
Isn't a wizard any more.

Abigail Golding (10)
Barnham Primary School, Barnham

Beachcomber

Monday I found a boot
Rust and salt leather
I gave it back to the sea to dance in
Tuesday I found a nugget of driftwood
Dead and damp
Gazing up at me like an ancient Aztec face
Wednesday I found a rat
Feathered and oily
Pecking at a salt-soaked chip
On Thursday I found another feathered rat
But this time there was no life in it
The bones were as empty as an abandoned cave
On Friday I found bladder-wrack
It was raindrops on a spiders web
I gave it back to the sea to wear.

Polly Sandiford-Ward
Carlton Hill Primary School, East Sussex

The Magnificent Monkey

My monkey is brown like a rusty piece of barbed wire
Found at the bottom of the sea
Brown like the wild grisly bears found in the forest
Brown like chocolate
His laugh is like a witch's laugh but from the other side of the world
My monkey is light like a running out light bulb
Found at the back of my stick house
Half of him is as bright as a teacher
His back shines like the sunshine above
His feet are cream like the chocolate dream
His legs are like flapping wings calling people from a distance
He loves the yellow banana.

Jessica Watters (9)
Christchurch CE School, St Leonards On Sea

The Magnificent Owl

My owl is as brown as a shimmering rock
Brown as a rusty chain on a bike
His hoot is like a whistle on a train
My owl is as brown as a plank of wood
His rough feathers shine in the moonlight
My owl sways to and fro
This way and that way
His eyes are like fire burning in a house
My owl's head is as soft as velvet
Half of the day he is as white as snow
And the other half of the day he is as dark as the midnight clouds
He resembles a piece of tar.

Lorenza Colosi (9)
Christchurch CE School, St Leonards On Sea

The Magnificent Dove

My dove is white like the sea froth in the water
As white as the egg white
White like a sheet of paper
His cooing noise, like people calling from far away
My dove is light like an exploding bomb
His back shines like a blizzard of snow
His brow is feathered like an Indian head dress
He resembles the sign of peace.

Billie Macleod Kotting (9)
Christchurch CE School, St Leonards On Sea

The Centipede

His legs are like bended straws
He eats rotten apple cores
His enemies have four paws

His shelters are under trees
He always finds enormous keys
His favourite band is The Black Eyed Peas.

Joshua Keeling (9)
Christchurch CE School, St Leonards On Sea

The Monkey

Monkeys swing from tree to tree
Picking off swarming fleas
As the furry monkey starts to sneeze

They only eat bananas for food
Sometimes they get in a gruesome mood
Because the zoo keepers just got sued.

James Western (9)
Christchurch CE School, St Leonards On Sea

Winter Nights

Snowflakes all around
All animals go in for shelter
Birds flutter up high to protect their little ones
Deep snow covers the ground

Whistling wind howls
Every night through the trees
Muffled footsteps through the snow
Deep snow covers the ground

Morning breaks through the sky
While night dies
Children come out to play
Now and again every day.

Whistling wind howls
Every night through the trees
Muffled footsteps through the snow
Deep snow covers the ground.

Alice Dyer (9)
Christchurch CE School, St Leonards On Sea

The Ancient Castle

The ancient castle stands near a forest
The doors creep open
Shadows lurking around

Eyes staring at you
So many rooms you don't know where to go
You can't see because there is no light

They say when the half moon is up in the sky
The ancient castle fades away
Never to be seen till morning.

Josephine Wright (9)
Christchurch CE School, St Leonards On Sea

The Naming Of The Cats

One is covered all over with black
With shiny, ruby red eyes
And she likes to sleep in a black sack
And she peeps out of corners and spies
I think we shall call her this
I think we shall call her that
Now, don't you think that Sookey
Is a nice name for a cat?

Amy Mitchell (9)
Christchurch CE School, St Leonards On Sea

The Mantis

Claws like knives
Armour like hard pies
But he has no sighs

He's the chief of the bug gang
When he's angry he goes off with a bang
'And I believe I can fly' he sang.

Tom Lewis (9)
Christchurch CE School, St Leonards On Sea

The Bull

My bull's horns are sharp and pointy like knives sticking together
Replacing horns and put on a bull's head.
Running faster and faster towards his prey
He scatters and rips his prey and tears his prey
In a couple of mouthfuls he has eaten his prey
He storms back home like thunder and lightning, striking together.

Silvana Kroni (9)
Christchurch CE School, St Leonards On Sea

The Night Rises, The Light Falls

The light falls
As the darkness calls
The sky turns brown
As darkness creeps around the town
The night rises, the light falls

The wind pushes with its hands
The water grumbling on top of the sands
Yes that happens while I watch the moon
I hope I'll be able to meet the sun soon
The night rises, the light falls

I hope the sky can show me more
As I walk across the shore
I would put up a fight
To see the beautiful light
The night rises, the light falls.

Ben Pierce (9)
Christchurch CE School, St Leonards On Sea

World At War

W ar is getting out of hand
O range flames burn throughout the land
R aging soldiers killing and shooting
L ots of people stealing and looting
D igging children screaming for shelter

W earing badges and fighting Hitler
A rguing and hanging all over the place
R unning at an extremely fast pace

T errible torture in the war
W inston Churchill making the law
O ver now.

Yolanda Rumball (9)
Christchurch CE School, St Leonards On Sea

The Ancient Castle

When the sun sets, the sand monster rises above the sand and roars
He goes into the castle and sees what's inside
But never keeps anyone alive

The castle is black with white arrows and trees touching the roof
The windows are covered in grey wood and shining paper
But still you can see inside

When it turns morning, the sand monster goes back
To it's hard, raggedy sand and stays all day
When it turns sun set again he does the same

He guards his castle all night long
Stays there for eight hours
He goes back to his raggedy sand and never returns.

Rachel Aylward (9)
Christchurch CE School, St Leonards On Sea

The Unicorn

My unicorn's horn is like a helter-skelter
White as snow stands her long silky mane
Her hooves are as shiny as silver crystals

Her eyes sparkle like the moonlit stars
Her legs are long and thin
Her name is starlight.

Olivia Baird-Piper (9)
Christchurch CE School, St Leonards On Sea

Happy Cinquain

Happy
Happy is good
Happy helps you to laugh
If you are sad cheer yourself up
Ha ha!

Freya Katherine Danes (8)
Firle CE Primary School, Lewes

Where Do We Go?

When the moon is out
And the sun is in
Don't fear the darkness
Just start to sing

Make the light
To see the door
That leads to heaven
Where you'll have trouble no more

Your soul will find
What's behind that door
It's golden it's glistening
Heaven.

Jack Rosewarne (9)
Firle CE Primary School, Lewes

The One And Only

Ryan is tall
Edward is small
Sam is quick
Ben is slick
Fred is mad
Dan is glad
Jack is wacky
Matt is happy
I am different
From all the rest
Pleased to meet you
I'm the best.

Noah Marsh (8)
Firle CE Primary School, Lewes

Where Do We Go?

I don't know
Where we go
Do we go up
Or do we go down
Don't worry
I'm still here
I don't know
Where we go

Why ask me
You go and see
Don't be scared
I'm still here
I don't know
Where we go
Through the clouds
Up in the sky
A bird's eye view
I see you
I don't know
Where we go

I don't know
Where we go
Do we go up
Or do we go down
Don't worry
I'm still here
I don't know
Where we go.

Lisken Jellings (9)
Firle CE Primary School, Lewes

Swimming

Diving
Arriving

Splash
Splish

Slippy
Wippy

Crash
Dash

Super
Duper

Swooping
Looping

Splashing
Crashing

Sophia Blee (9)
Firle CE Primary School, Lewes

Lonely – Cinquains

Lonely
Always alone
Never funny or sad
Just because you're always alone
Ignored

At night
Never sleeping
In a sad straw haystack
Tossing, turning in a dead world
Confused.

Edith Burns (9)
Firle CE Primary School, Lewes

What Is Death Like?

What is death like?
Is it long
Is it short
Is it peaceful
Is it scary?

What do you do?
Go straight up
Or go straight down?
What is it like?

Matthew Ashton Tye (9)
Firle CE Primary School, Lewes

When You Are Alone . . .

You feel as if you've left the worlds
You're hiding from the people
You start to get sleepy
It's all peaceful around you
The words of the earth are a blur
You feel as if you're floating in space

And the world does not matter.

Zannia Kidd (8)
Firle CE Primary School, Lewes

Alone

I'm alone, I need somebody
I'm lonely I need my friends
I'm alone I need you
I'm alone I worry
I'm alone I need my mum.

Ryan Peirce (8)
Firle CE Primary School, Lewes

What Happens

Is it dangerous?
I don't think so
Why should it be?
I don't know
Is it blank?
Yes

What happens?
Will I think all the time?
I don't know.

Ben Morris (9)
Firle CE Primary School, Lewes

The Mountain High

Climb, climb the mountain high
Touch the clouds and see the sky
Feel the wind against you blow
See the fields far, far below

Climb, climb the mountain high
Touch the clouds and see the sky
Feel the wind in your hair
It pushes you back into the air

Climb, climb the mountain high
Touch the clouds and see the sky
Feel the wind against your eyes
It blinds you like the summer sky

Climb, climb the mountain high
Touch the clouds and see the sky
Feel the wind against you blow
See the fields far, far below.

Zac Burchell (11)
Heron Way Primary School, Horsham

Eight-Legged Chaos

The spider's gone up the curtains
Abi's got a scare
Dad is being really brave
Mum is standing on the chair!

Now the spider's on the ceiling
Crawling round and round
My little sister's squealing
But now the spider's found!

Grandad let the spider go!
Nanny tripped and fell
Everyone's rushing to and fro
They didn't hear Grandad yell:

'The spider's heading to the door
Followed by the cat'
'Oh no,' said Grandad
So that's the end of that!

Lara Cardew (11)
Heron Way Primary School, Horsham

A Crescent Moon

A bright crescent moon is a comfy seat
An interesting shaped cheese for you to eat

So far away from Earth
That you'd only hear a mutter
From the man in the moon
Who lives on cheese and butter

He eats it with bread
Before he settles down to bed
On a moon shaped like a hook
That makes you want to look

Because it's such an interesting sight
On a pitch dark night!

Nicola Carter (11)
Heron Way Primary School, Horsham

Dawn

The sky was bright with diamond stars
And sweeping hills rolled on either side
The moon was a sickle in the sky
Frost stiffened the grass and the wild wind cried
Svelte deer pawed the frozen ground
Their black eyes round and bright
Their breath leaving frosty iron clouds
Carved in the cold of the moonlight
Empty silence was cupped in the hills
The air heavy with frost and riddled with staring eyes
Shadows swarmed and flooded the land
And even moonlight was tied back with midnight ties.

Until the sun filtered the dark
Traced detail into the night
Split down to its blinding core
And threw out its raging light
Until the blackbird's call
The thrush's song, the skylark's tune
Tore the silence and echoed down and down
Until all around the song was strewn
Then the trees were draped in golden light
And the frost revealed its fires
Silence hung like drab rags in the air
And mist rose in twisting spires
As dawn echoed throughout the land.

Jenifer Bloomfield (11)
Heron Way Primary School, Horsham

Christmas

C hristmas is the time of year
   When all the men drink pints of beer
H olly and mistletoe hanging in the hall
   A picture of Santa upon the wall
R un downstairs and look with glee
   All the presents under the Christmas tree
I t's Christmas Eve in the house
   Not a person was stirring not even the mouse
S hout for joy - it's Christmas Day
   Give three cheers, hip, hip and hooray
T able full of food and drink
   What on earth will Santa think?
M ince pies and Christmas treats
   At the table - no spare seats
A nd now it's time for presents, whoopee!
   Start with the ones under the tree
S now is coming really fast
   A white Christmas - how long will it last?

Emma Brown (11)
Heron Way Primary School, Horsham

The Seaside

The rugged grey-black cliffs as hard as cold steel
The seashells as beautiful as a see-through sparkling diamond
The blue sea is as clear as a crystal glistening in the sunlight
The seaweed is as green and as slimy
As a slug getting swept up by the big rising waves
The fish is like a shimmering rainbow shining in the light blue sky
The crabs are like a red hot chilli pepper burning in the red hot sun
The sand is covered with jagged grey coloured rocks
And with colourful seashells on the high top hillside
The waves are like turquoise horses tossing their manes.

Laura Brooke-Simmons (11)
Heron Way Primary School, Horsham

My Body

Brains, brains connected to your veins
Head, head I keep it in my garden shed
Tongue, tongue saying 'hi', to my lung
Mouth, mouth heading to the south
Nose, nose smelling my toes
Eyes, eyes looking at my ties
Arms, arms really harms
Chest, chest touching my vest
Tummy, tummy eats lots of gummy
Legs, legs always begs
Feet, feet absorb the heat
Toes, toes washed by the garden hose
Heart, heart likes jam tart
Rib, rib always hid
Bladder, bladder climbs a ladder
Lungs, lungs always hums.

Nick Freeman (11)
Heron Way Primary School, Horsham

Sadness

Sadness is a cold dark grey colour like a cloud on a stormy day
Sadness follow you everywhere like a gloomy mist
Which lingers over a graveyard
Sadness is like a moth-eaten coat which has not seen
The light of day in a long time
Sadness is when you feel like you are on your own
With no one around you
Sadness is like you are in a dark room
Left with nothing but an eerie sound
But then the light returns
And chases all the clouds away.

Phoebe Douthwaite-Hodges (11)
Heron Way Primary School, Horsham

The Rich In Tudor Times

In Tudor times
There were the rich
Who had posh names like Sir Mitch

They lived in big houses
With women who wore pink frilly blouses

They had lots of money
And made their own honey

Which they ate with bread
During breakfast in bed

Whilst out and about
They wouldn't dare to call or shout
For they had an image to maintain
While riding on horseback across the moorland plain

When holding grand dinner parties
They were sure to give each guest some smarties
But the guests said, 'Good gracious what are these?'
The hosts replied, 'A gift from us - take them please'

While seeing to some workers
You see those same lurkers
The ones you have to shoo away
Almost every single day.

Natassja Etherington (11)
Heron Way Primary School, Horsham

The Owl

White and brown and having fun
Looking for it's prey at night
It has long sharp claws and a sharp beak
Eyes that light up when it's dark
It is fluffy when you touch it
It is not good when you touch it.

Catherine Bevan (11)
Heron Way Primary School, Horsham

Argument

First it's kicking
Then we shout
'I don't want you in my room, get out!'
Then it's screaming, trying to punch
Then Mum and Dad say
'Blimey, you two are a right old bunch
Arguing over the silliest thing!'
Then the doorbell gives a loud shrill ring
I run down the stairs to the door
Tripped over the rug and felt quite sore
It really hurt and I started to cry
Then my brother called me 'stupid!'
As he ran by
I got up and called him 'a smelly old dog'
He shouted and called me a 'revolting hog!'
I opened the door and it was Grandpa
Standing on the doorstep with Grandma
He said, 'What are you two fighting about?'
I started to scream and I started to shout
'He gets to do everything first - it's not fair'
Then grandpa sat us down and said
'Cor, you two are a right old pair
Now let's make everything calm and fair'
He made us both say sorry
And everything was alright
Until the next day when
He splattered me with porridge
And we started to scream and shout!

Jonathan Knapman (10)
Heron Way Primary School, Horsham

A Spider's Viewpoint

How would you feel if -
Every day was a struggle for life?
Every day you were running away from screaming humans
While dodging feet, trying to make you feel part of the ground

How would you feel if -
You had just spent hours making your home
Then massive hands destroy it in seconds and you fall to the ground
Plummeting like a stone?

How would you feel if -
You had just picked up the threads of a broken life
And just started to rebuild your home, your *whole* world
And it crashes back down on you just like a meteorite hitting a planet
Your planet

How would you feel if -
You were searching for a place to live and
A ball came and squashed your flat?

Well?
How would you feel if -
You were me?

Robert Potter (11)
Heron Way Primary School, Horsham

The Full Moon

A full moon is a ball, bouncing high over the fence
A full moon is a balloon, floating around the world
Seeing the wonders of the planet
A full moon is a target which a French longbow man is
Aiming his thin, narrow, light arrow at it
A full moon is a fruit sitting in the bowl
That is in space with the other fruits which are the planets
A full moon is a glowing shield which a warrior lost in battle
A full moon is a circular saw, waiting to cut deeply into wood.

Glenn Hunter (11)
Heron Way Primary School, Horsham

Beep! Beep!

Beep! Beep! Get out of the way
Cars hooting hour upon hour
The road is now a big delay
An empty road that's all they desire

The chaos gathers on the street
Cars moving inches apart
A frustrated driver sits in his seat
Engines revving, ready to start

Leaning out of their open windows
Shouting at the car ahead
The cars on the other side struggle on
Cars crossing into different lanes instead.

Tessa Smith (11)
Heron Way Primary School, Horsham

Spiders

Spiders
Horrible and black
Crawling out of every crack
I think they're scary
Horrible and hairy
I hate them

Spiders
Beady eyes
Searching for flies
Spinning their webs
With eight hairy legs
I hate them.

Oscar Smith (11)
Heron Way Primary School, Horsham

A Cheetah Poem

A cheetah is a fast feline
Running in and out of the vines
It zooms so fast to catch it's prey
Before dusk at the end of the day

 A cheetah has spots on it's back
When it's running it's easy to lose track
A cheetah can go 75mph
At that time it gives a lot of power

A cheetah can creep and crawl very slowly
So it can surprise it's enemies and foe
It can also leap and jump up very high
And it prowls around waiting for it's prey to pass by.

Jack Stocker (10)
Heron Way Primary School, Horsham

Monkey

Swinging from branch to branch
Stopping a moment to have some lunch
Three bananas he quickly swallows
Then a mate passes by, so he turns and follows
Grabbed his tail and made him yell
Just before he lost his balance and fell
Tumbling to the ground with a bump
But he's not hurt, he's up with a jump
Then his mum grabs his arm
She doesn't want him to come to any harm
On her back the ride is bumpy
But it's safe for a baby monkey.

Samantha Thornton-Rice (11)
Heron Way Primary School, Horsham

Kitten

Cute, cuddly kittens like to sleep
And likes to play hide and seek!

Playful, active kittens like to play with balls of wool
And enjoys scampering after a blowing leaf too

Soft, colourful kittens are all different colours
And it's not people they think they're cute too!

Scared, frightened kittens get scared easily
Even looking at themselves!

Small, furry kittens can get lost
Especially under a pile of laundry!

Funny, curious, silly kittens are always up to mischief
And never seem to stop finding any!

Anna Wilson (11)
Heron Way Primary School, Horsham

Spider

Prickly spiky
Hairy and small
In the cracks in the garden wall
And in it's fangs, death it keeps
On top of a swaying web it sleeps
Wrapping it's prey with diamond thread
Sucking it's juices until it's dead
With spindly legs it scuttles and leaps
You move your foot
For eternity it sleeps.

Mark McKinney (11)
Heron Way Primary School, Horsham

Spiders

Spinning out webs all day long, a human comes then the web is gone
Patiently waiting to catch a fly, hoping that something tasty will
come by
I like it in this cold dark room, I really hope some food will come soon
Dare I move? Will I be seen? The worst is when they start to clean
Every one finds me very scary, just because I've got long legs and
I'm hairy
Running, scurrying across the floor, hoping I'll make it to the door
Safe at last I need a rest, but scaring people is what I do best!

Alice Stennett (11)
Heron Way Primary School, Horsham

Fairies

Fairies are so tiny
They're tiny all the time
They creep into your bedroom and give you a little surprise
The tooth fairy is the tiniest out of all that's ever been
But listen very carefully and you might just hear
The flutter of the dainty wings so light
And hear the fairies singing the secret song of the night
As they fly through the dark and glimmering sky
Wish the glowing bright moon and the sparkling stars
Help their magic work
With their magic wands.

Emily Grimble (9)
Hoddern Junior School, Peacehaven

My Lazy Dad

My dad is very, very lazy
He drives me up the wall
I do not want my dad to be lazy, no, no, no
If I want a drink he won't let me have a drink.

Bethany Donegan (8)
Hoddern Junior School, Peacehaven

Ted

Ted, ted
Lost his head
Rolled on the cat

Ted, ted
In his shed
Making a bat

Ted, ted
Wants to go to bed
But instead he sat on his mat

Ted, ted
Went to bed
And stroked the cat

Ted, ted
Wet the bed
Weed over his new bat

Ted, ted
With his head
Kissing his cat.

Annie Brooks (9)
Hoddern Junior School, Peacehaven

Spring

Spring is the best
Spring is in the west
Spring is fun dancing in the sun
Spring is when the bees come out
Buzz, buzz, fuzz, fuzz
In spring, birds flying up, up, up and away
Flap flap flap and I have to go away.

Saffron Amis (8)
Hoddern Junior School, Peacehaven

Surprises In The Garden

A garden is full of wonderful surprises
Things jump out at you when you least expect them to
Like when you are looking in a big bushy tree
Out jumps a frog. *Ribit!*
When you smell the lovely scent of a lavender bush or a lemon tree
Out flies a bumble bee
It stings you on the nose
Bzzzzz ouch!

In the morning the garden is silent and as still as can be
In the garden at midday when the sun is shining
And you are laughing with all those insects jumping out at you
In the evening the sun is low and then all those surprises are still
In the morning everything that I have ever said
In this poem is going to happen all over again.

Grace Tobin (9)
Hoddern Junior School, Peacehaven

My Bath Poem

Please remember don't forget
Never leave the bathroom wet
Nor leave the soap still in the water
That's the thing you never ought'er
And as you like to be told
Never leave the hot run cold
Nor leave the towel upon the floor
Or keep the bath an hour or more
When other folks are waiting for one
Just say, 'I'm not done'
If you really do that thing
You better remember to sing

Laura Day (9)
Hoddern Junior School, Peacehaven

Holiday In The Sun

Holiday in the sun
Is so much fun
Working together
To get the weather
Ever so fine
As a dime
You jump in the pool
To get cool
You put on your sun cream
To keep away from the sun beam
So that's my holiday
In the sun!

Shelby Teale (9)
Hoddern Junior School, Peacehaven

Daydreams

Miss Hayes thinks I'm reading
But I'm swimming with blue whales
I am lying in mid-air or
Riding in a kangaroo's pouch
I have a ride on a unicorn and
Get to meet an angel.

Miss Hayes thinks I'm working
But I'm sitting on a firework travelling in the sky
I'm talking to a rat or
Walking up the wall
I have a giant pizza
And have a snooze in bed.

Rhianna Light (8)
Pebsham CP School, Bexley-on-Sea

Fangel

I wish I had a Fangel,
It would be so cool,
A cross between a fairy
And an angel too.

She would grant all of my wishes,
I'd roll around in gold,
She'd give me everything I wanted,
Never to be sold.

She'd fly me everywhere I wanted,
Flying through the stars,
See the wonders of Pluto,
Jupiter and Mars.

Her name will be Sabrina,
She'll be so precious to me,
I'll love her until the end of time,
For eternity.

Kirsty Hoggins (11)
Pebsham CP School, Bexley-on-Sea

My Best Friend

She's always there
Because she cares.
Oh yes . . . she's Zoe
She's always funny
She's cute like a bunny
Oh yes . . . she's Zoe
She loves boys
But hates toys
Oh yes . . . she's Zoe
She's always crazy
She's sometimes lazy
Just like me
Oh yes . . . *she's Zoe!*

Hannah Rancic (10)
Pebsham CP School, Bexley-on-Sea

Snowboarding

S nowing at night,
N ight has passed, time to get ready.
O ver the moon with excitement,
W ondering what mountain to ride.
B oard in hand,
O llie, my little bro, is a beginner at this sport.
A nd now I am at the top of the mountain,
R iding down the mountain with my brother.
D odging rocks and trees as I go,
I mproving skills every minute.
N o going back.
G ot to go! How annoying!

Adam Hollands (10)
Pebsham CP School, Bexley-on-Sea

Wellie Monster

There's a monster in the forest
Slimy as a slug.
Grabbing you from underground
Like a person in a coffin.
Knowing your every move like a hypnotist.
Eyes like balls of fire wanting to grab you.
Tripping you up.
There's a monster in the forest
And you wouldn't know when he would come out again!

Billy Reeves (10)
Pebsham CP School, Bexley-on-Sea

Lightning

It has a glow which lights up the sky.
It makes the grey clouds spit out light.
The lightning flashes zigzags of silver.
Whips of light, angry cracks, deadly electric.

Jordan Byford (9)
Pebsham CP School, Bexley-on-Sea

Kittens

Loveable like a newborn baby
Sweet like chocolate
Furry like a teddy
Playful like a puppy
Cute like a dolphin
Precious like my family
Cheering me up when I'm sad or lonely
Eyes glittering like twinkling stars in the sky
Black like a hole
So I shall call him Midnight.

Hazel Holland (11)
Pebsham CP School, Bexley-on-Sea

A Poem To Be Said Silently

It was so quite
That I heard a leaf let go of the tree.
It was so quiet
That I heard a plant crackling out of its seed.
It was so quiet
That I could hear the water sitting in the pipes.

Cassandra Kourti (8)
Pebsham CP School, Bexley-on-Sea

School

School, suicide in a building.
School, boring like a banana.
School, learning all day and we never get away.
School, scary as a monster in the dark.
School, tests like SATs make you shake at the sight of the word.
School, biting you in the head
Then you'll be dead!

Mustafa Hamed (11)
Pebsham CP School, Bexley-on-Sea

Daydreams

Miss Hayes thinks I'm reading
But I'm riding in a kangaroo's pouch.
I'm dancing on the moon
Or floating in the stars.
I have danced with the fairies
And played with the elves.

Miss Hayes thinks I'm working quietly
But I'm soaking in the bath.
I'm sitting on a sandy beach
Or swimming in the sea.
I have swum with dolphins
And the fish have played with me.

Elle Lakin (9)
Pebsham CP School, Bexley-on-Sea

Daydreams

Miss Hayes thinks I'm watching TV
But I'm talking to a bear.
I'm walking up the wall
Or I'm lying in mid-air.
I'm swimming in a massive cake
And then I am talking with a Chinese rat.

Miss Hayes thinks I'm listening
But I'm swimming in a milkshake.
I'm making my friend turn into a pig
Or I'm swimming in dried mud with ants.
I'm having a mud bath with a bear.

Joshua Page (8)
Pebsham CP School, Bexley-on-Sea

Summer

Summer
It's the best time of year
Summer
It's scorching
Summer
Going down the beach with friends
Summer
Getting a sun tan
Summer
Playing in the park, having picnics
Summer
Having summer parties
Summer
Ice cream melting in my hands going everywhere
Summer
Getting up early with excitement
Summer
Eating dinner outside with your family
Summer
Not wanting to go in when you are asked
Summer
Playing in the swimming pool with friends
Summer
The best time of year
Summer
It will soon sadly end.

Zoe Henderson (11)
Pebsham CP School, Bexley-on-Sea

Spooky

Ghosts are moaning,
Zombies are groaning,
People are screaming,
Lights are beaming.
Screaming more,
At the door.
Zombies are showing,
There's no sign of slowing,
They just keep on going,
Throwing and throwing,
Boom!
There's a noise in the tomb,
Running and running,
Keep on running,
A mumble,
A tumble,
With a rumble,
Through the tomb,
To their doooooommmm!
They all go.

Ben Watts (11)
Pebsham CP School, Bexley-on-Sea

Bone People

I can see a nasty dog
Is it his or is it yours?
I can see its nasty teeth
I can see its nasty nose
Is it going to follow him
Or is it going to follow you?
It is not going to follow him
It is going to follow you
I can see it sprinting up the hill
Now it's munching you
Now it's buried you.

Jordan Gildersleeve (10)
Pebsham CP School, Bexley-on-Sea

Spiders

Black spiders, hairy spiders,
Big spiders, creepy spiders,
Crawling up your arm
And tickling you.

Freaky spiders, scary spiders,
Wandering in your garden
And making lots of cobwebs in your house,
Making you scared,
Giving you nightmares.

Marcus Winchester (10)
Pebsham CP School, Bexley-on-Sea

A Poem To Be Said Silently

It was so quiet
I could hear my feet growing.
It was so quiet
I could hear the ladybird moving on the flower.
It was so quiet
I could hear the worm under the ground.
It was so quiet
I could hear a turtle walking on the sand.

Samuel Russell (9)
Pebsham CP School, Bexley-on-Sea

Love

Love is nice like rice and can break like thin ice,
Love is spoilt and sometimes it's loyal,
Love is painful instead of playful,
Love is lonely making you think of land all green
With no one in sight,
Love is beautiful like a lovely waterfall.

Michelle Wadey (11)
Pebsham CP School, Bexley-on-Sea

Spooky Tombs

In a tomb on the walls,
Booby traps are about to fall.

Beware of the mummies' curse,
That's about to burst!
Whoever releases it will fall down dead!

Move on down a little bit more,
Ghosts and zombies are guarding a door.

Inside that room treasure you shall find,
Send the ghosts and zombies to sleep with a lullaby.

You fall down a ditch,
And get a stitch,
Lose the treasure
And you shall be annoyed.

James Clark (10)
Pebsham CP School, Bexley-on-Sea

Family

My family . . .
Cuddly like a big teddy bear.
Fun like a new board game.
Happy like a baby laughing!
Laughing like a happy hyena.
Caring like charities.
Cheerful like a tweety bird.
Loving and trusting.
Thoughtful like an owl.
Crazy like a parrot.
Caring, talking,
Special.

Holly Gearing (11)
Pebsham CP School, Bexley-on-Sea

Dolphins

Dolphins, cute as a teddy bear.
Cuddly as a baby.
Blue like the sea.
Jumpy like a springing frog.
Funny like a clown at the circus.
Precious like a golden crown.

Dolphins jump in and out of the sea.
Slimy like gunge!
Wet like when you're in a paddling pool.

Kayleigh Louise Dann (10)
Pebsham CP School, Bexley-on-Sea

Teachers

Technical like a computer,
Everybody listens,
Good at reading,
Chatters like chattering teeth,
Helps people learn,
Even lets you play,
Writes about your behaviour,
So look out or she might . . . bite!

Jamie Cowling (10)
Pebsham CP School, Bexley-on-Sea

A Poem To Be Said Silently

It was so quiet
I could hear my legs growing.
It was so quiet
I could hear the first drop of snow.
It was so quiet
I could hear my friend thinking.
It was so quiet
I could hear a feather fall on the ground.

Shannon Beeching (9)
Pebsham CP School, Bexley-on-Sea

A Poem Of Love

Love is a feeling
Everyone feels love.
Love makes the world go round!
Love is not *just* a feeling but a special thought to everyone.
Everyone has a different side to themselves.
Some feel happy about love
But sometimes love can spoil things.
Love comes from the heart,
It makes two people have a great life together.
You will know when you have found the right person,
Your heart starts to beat faster when you see them.
I feel *love* every day,
It helps me live my life.
Love!
Love is great!

Leanne Colvin (11)
Pebsham CP School, Bexley-on-Sea

My Mum

I'm glad I have a mum
My mum
No one else
My mum
No one horrible
My mum
Always caring
My mum
Very special
My mum
Always there
Forever mine
My mum.

Georgia Martin (10)
Pebsham CP School, Bexley-on-Sea

Love

Love makes everything right,
Makes you think, makes you fight
Through the hard things life gives you.

Love
Love is sometimes painful,
When love for him is still strong
But love for me has gone.

Love
Love's crazy,
Crazy as can be,
Makes you fall off your feet.

Love
Love's romantic,
Candlelit dinners
Makes you feel good.

Love
Love should be when someone's there all the time,
Helps make you feel -
Love's the best thing in the world!

April Grant (11)
Pebsham CP School, Bexley-on-Sea

A Mysterious Man

In the night a
Mysterious man
Wanders about at
The strike of dawn
A murderer is on the
Loose. Just knowing
He's out there gives
You the shivers.
He seeks
His prey.

Ryan Morgan (11)
Pebsham CP School, Bexley-on-Sea

James, The Boy Of My Dreams

He gives me confidence in all that I do,
He makes me feel happy when I'm blue.
When I'm lonesome he will comfort me
But best of all he makes me laugh,
Most times.

He's crazy and loving,
Funny, happy and shy.
His personality is great,
He's my type of guy.

I love him and always will,
James,
He is the boy of my dreams.

Amber Marie Hayler (11)
Pebsham CP School, Bexley-on-Sea

Ghosts

Ghosts, they are so scary
And they haunt you in your dreams.
They creep up behind you
So you run away and scream
Argh!
They come out of graves at night,
They scare you to death
So you huggle into your bed.
When you wake up you wouldn't want
To go to bed ever again.
You wouldn't want the night
To ever come again.

Sam Walters (11)
Pebsham CP School, Bexley-on-Sea

A Poem To Be Said Silently

It was so quiet
I could hear my eyeballs talk to my eyebrows.

It was so quiet
I heard the clock run out of batteries.

It was so quiet
I heard the seals squeal in the sea off the Arctic.

Keeley Pavlis (8)
Pebsham CP School, Bexley-on-Sea

Football, Football

Football, football, lovely football
Running down the wing
I cross the ball - *goal!*
My team is 1-0 up
Football, football, lovely football.

Running past players
Into the penalty box
Penalty! Yellow card
Then . . . *oops*, over the bar
Football, football, lovely football.

Into extra time, it's 1-1
30 seconds left
On the break - *foul!*
The last kick of the game
Goal, Lazio
Football, football, lovely football!

Martyn Durrant (11)
St Leonards CE Primary School, St Leonards-on-Sea

My Hamster

My hamster is called Coffee,
He likes to eat red treats.
His cage is black; one of the floors is yellow.

My hamster is called Coffee,
He likes to drink yoghurt and water.
His cage is black; one of the floors is green.

My hamster is called Coffee,
He likes to go on instead of in his wheel.
His cage is black; one of the floors is red.

Kelly Fairall (11)
St Leonards CE Primary School, St Leonards-on-Sea

The Bookshelf At School

The bookshelf at school
Is nothing at all
Like a bookshelf at Buckingham Palace
But if you look closely
You will most likely
See a book with only one page
So pick it up quick
(And don't take the mick)
'Cause this is just what it says.

Brook Tate (10)
St Leonards CE Primary School, St Leonards-on-Sea

My Rapping Rhyme

My name is Joel but my friends call me bowl.
I like shepherd's pie but my baby brother cries.
I skate downtown with the Queen's crown.
I have a cat that destroyed my hat.

Joel Phillips (11)
St Leonards CE Primary School, St Leonards-on-Sea

What I Like

I like football, going in goal,
I like cricket, don't like to bowl.
I support Arsenal,
Don't like Man U.
I support Arsenal, who do you?
I like, I like, I like.

I like Maths, really good at tables,
I like English, hard to start a story,
My favourite table is the nines,
Decimals, fractions,
Any calculations.
I like, I like, I like.

Jack Torode (11)
St Leonards CE Primary School, St Leonards-on-Sea

Chocolate

Chocolate is dreamy,
It's luscious and creamy,
I could eat it all day,
But then my mum did say,
'Don't eat too much of that,
Unless you want to be fat!'
I thought about what she said,
And hid the chocolate under my bed.
Chocolate is dreamy,
It's so luscious and creamy!

Lily Bostanabad (10)
St Leonards CE Primary School, St Leonards-on-Sea

My Favourite Food

My favourite food is chocolate,
My worst is hot and spicy,
It makes my taste buds tizzle
But chocolate makes them wizzle.

Yummy!
Yummy!
Yummy!
In my tummy!

I most like different sweets,
I really hate chicken curry,
Everyone has a favourite,
So write a poem like me, but hurry!

Yummy!
Yummy!
Yummy!
In my tummy!

What's *your* favourite?

Katie Kirkby (11)
St Leonards CE Primary School, St Leonards-on-Sea

Some Cats

Some cats are black,
Some cats are brown and white
And I have never seen a green cat,
Have you?
Some cats are ginger,
Some cats are gold,
Some cats are silver,
Grey, white and silver.
So what is your favourite animal?
Well, my favourite animal is a . . .
Cat.

Emma Rose (11)
St Leonards CE Primary School, St Leonards-on-Sea

Chocolate Makes Me Dreamy

Chocolate makes me dreamy
In every single way,
Especially when it's creamy
I could eat it every day.

Chocolate to me is so rich and soft
I am glad I have lots stored in the loft.

Chocolate makes me dreamy
In every single way,
Especially when it's creamy
I could eat it every day.

But don't tell my mum that
Because she will say,
'Do you want to get fat?'
And I will have to obey.

Chocolate makes me dreamy
In every single way,
Especially when it's creamy
I could eat it every day.

Daniella Ratnarajah (10)
St Leonards CE Primary School, St Leonards-on-Sea

Everything I Like

I like football, just saved a penalty,
I'm fond of cricket, going to bowl,
I support Arsenal, don't like Man U,
My favourite player's Thierry Henry,
What about you?
I find pizza pleasant, don't find mushrooms pleasant.
My favourite colour's red, hate going to bed.
Everything I like, everything I like,
I enjoy chicken but I don't enjoy stew.

Ryan Couchman (11)
St Leonards CE Primary School, St Leonards-on-Sea

My Grandad

My granddad has a very big belly,
He is always watching Countdown on the telly,
He sits in his big, puffy chair eating toffees,
While drinking hot coffees.

He sometimes does the washing up,
Although he thinks it a pain,
Because he says he gets rough hands -
I don't think it's true.

When I touch his hands they feel soft,
He just laughs and sits in his chair,
And in no time he will fall asleep,
But I still know he is not telling the truth about his gentle hands.

Lauren Fuller (11)
St Leonards CE Primary School, St Leonards-on-Sea

When Mum Went Shopping

Coats on, get the keys, through the door,
In the car, out the car, lock the door,
Through the gates, get the trolley,
Race to the left and grab the bread,
Race to the right, speed to the left,
Picks up the crisps, get the milk,
Aisle 13, race to the drinks,
Get a lot of drinks,
Coke, beer, lemonade,
To the till, hurry up,
Beep, beep, beep,
200 things go through the till,
Oh no, I haven't got enough money!

Georgina Parlour (11)
St Leonards CE Primary School, St Leonards-on-Sea

Dogs Hate Frogs

Dogs hate frogs
But frogs love dogs,
On the moon,
On the moon.

Dogs can't breathe
But frogs can breathe,
On the moon,
On the moon.

So take them home
And give the dog a bone
And give the frog a fly
And hope he doesn't cry,
On the moon,
    The moon,
    The moooooon.

Ivan Miller (11)
St Leonards CE Primary School, St Leonards-on-Sea

My Little Brother

My little brother is very, very weird
My mum thinks he's tough
My dad thinks he's rough
But I have always known him to be weird.

He watches telly whilst eating pink jelly
But he is always singing to the rhythm of R Kelly.

My brother's a pain
He can be angelic
But he's not always that way.

I've told you the worst
He could be okay
But in 6 months' time he will have to obey.

Shani White (11)
St Leonards CE Primary School, St Leonards-on-Sea

Living A Dream

I was walking down the street,
Living a dream.
Tappin' my feet,
And this is what I've seen.

A whale with wings,
A plodding poodle,
And an elephant with just one eye.

I was walking down the street,
Living a dream.
Tappin' my feet,
And this is what I've seen.

A bloated baboon,
A singing squirrel,
And a tiger wearing a tie.

Matthew Viney (10)
St Leonards CE Primary School, St Leonards-on-Sea

Mory

Over, under, inside and down.
Mory loves to swim all around.
He looks like a snake, could be a fish.
To be your best friend is his only wish.
Over, under, inside and down.
He might shrivel up if you put him on the ground.

Can you guess what he is?
Can you guess what he is?

Yes!
He is the wormly, electric eel.
Yes!
You guessed, you guessed!

Austin Delamaine (11)
St Leonards CE Primary School, St Leonards-on-Sea

Poppy

Poppy is a rabbit.
She loves to go out and hop around the garden,
She loves her carrot as much as me.

Poppy is a rabbit.
She is soft and sweet, she is as kind as a fairy
And not one bit scary.

Poppy is a rabbit.
She will always be the same
And I will love her forever.

Kirsty Alice Sinden (10)
St Leonards CE Primary School, St Leonards-on-Sea

Dreams

They can scare,
They can delight
And only come at night
Into a child's and adult's mind,
Where they find
The pieces of tasting, smelling, hearing and touching.
The mind is like a book where dreams can look.

Hannah Crouch (10)
St Leonards CE Primary School, St Leonards-on-Sea

Brighton Pier

Starlings like a flock of sheep,
Birds cry as the raindrops fall.
Swooping together through the rusty pier.
Sunset falls as waves crash against the shore.
Birds swooping through the rusty, old pier
Like a wave crashing on the muddy beach.

Kayleigh Thurmer (11)
St Mark's CE School, Brighton

Alphabet Poem

(An extract A - N)

A is for Amy
Who is really cheeky.
    A B C
B is for Bethany
Who is really sneaky.
    A B C
C is for Charlotte
Who is really peaky.
    A B C
D is for Dan
Who is really creepy.
    A B C
E is for Emma
Who chases after Fred.
    A B C
F is for Fred
Who wets his bed.
    A B C
G is for George
Who loves to play on the beach.
    A B C
H is for Hayley
Who hates to play hide and seek.
    A B C
I is for Isabelle
Who loves Maths.
    A B C
J is for Jack
Who really fancies Cath.
    A B C
K is for Kayleigh
Who loves to play with babies.
    A B C
L is for Lacey
Who hates Hayley.
    A B C

M is for Matt
Who likes to sit on a cat.
   A B C
N is for Nicole
Who bought a new bat.

Esme Cole (9)
St Mark's CE School, Brighton

Alphabet Poem
(An extract A - I)

A is for Amy
Who likes hats.
   A B C
B is for Ben
Who has lots of cats.
   A B C
C is for Chloe
Who likes to dance.
   A B C
D is for Danni
Who likes to take a chance.
   A B C
E is for Emma
Who has a good voice.
   A B C
F is for Fred
Who makes a good choice.
   A B C
G is for Georgia
Who likes to take a dip in a pool.
   A B C
H is for Hannah
Who never goes to school.
   A B C
I is for Isabelle
Who loves to teach.

Emma Holdway (9)
St Mark's CE School, Brighton

Alphabet Poem

(An extract A - N)

A is for Amber
Who likes to play.

B is for Bennie
Who likes to run all day.

C is for Cathy
Who always has a chance.

D is for Dannie
Who likes to dance.

E is for Ellie
Who likes to cook.

F is for Fred
Who likes to read a book.

G is for Georgie
Who fights like a duck.

H is for Harry
Who has all the luck.

I is for iris
Who holds everyone's hand.

J is for Jack
Who made up a band.

K is for Kerry
Who always spins around.

L is for Lisa
Who always has a pound.

M is for Mark
Who is nice.

N is for Nikki
Who eats all the rice.

Kayleigh Rosario (9)
St Mark's CE School, Brighton

Alphabet Poem

(An extract A, - N)

A is for Annie
Who talks all day.

B is for Ben
Who likes to play.

C is for Claire
Who is eight.

D is for Daniel
Who is always late.

E is for Ellie
Who takes a chance.

F is for Frankie
Who likes to dance.

G is for Georgia
Who has lots of hats.

H is for Harvey
Who likes cats.

I is for Isabelle
Who is nice.

J is for Jamie
Who likes rice.

K is for Kirsty
Who has a swimming pool.

L is for Lisa
Who never goes to school.

M is for Martin
Who is very bad.

N is for Nikkie
Who is always sad.

Chloe Openshaw (8)
St Mark's CE School, Brighton

Alphabet Poem

(An extract A - N)

A is for Amanda
Who combs her hair.

B is for Ben
Who likes a ripe pear.

C is for Courtney
Who is always bossy.

D is for Derek
Who's hair is all glossy.

E is for Esme
Who loves her new clothes.

F is for Fred
Who has smelly toes.

G is for Georgia
Who's always nosy.

H is for Helen
Whose cheeks are always rosy.

I is for Ian
Who likes to play games.

J is for Jack
Whose best friend is James.

K is for Kelly
Who likes wobbly jelly.

L is for Levi
Who likes his green wellies.

M is for Molly
Who has a pretty dolly.

N is for Nicole
Who has a new brolly.

Charlotte Rolf (9)
St Mark's CE School, Brighton

Alphabet Poem

(An extract A - I)

A is for Amber
Who loves to play.

B is for Ben
Who loves to run all day.

C is for Clare
Who loves to dance.

D is for Dianna
Who always has the chance.

E is for Ellie
Who's always on the run.

F is for Frankie
Who loves to eat a bun.

G is for Georgia
Who loves to sing.

H is for Hayley
Who sees the king.

I is for Isabelle
Who's always cool.

Zoe Fortune (8)
St Mark's CE School, Brighton

Brighton Starlings

Starlings swooping in the starlit sky.
Brown birds blossoming feathers.
Starlings look like a swarm of bees.
Travelling flocks day or night.

Starlings scream helpful screams.
Stars moving across the sky.
Sleeping on the pier above the water
Or swooping at the creaks of rust,
Brown as a tree trunk.

Reece Taylor
St Mark's CE School, Brighton

Alphabet Poem

(An extract A,- F)

A is for Andrew
Who breaks into cars.

B is for Ben
Who eats all the chocolate bars.

C is for Calum
Who has a blue house.

D is for David
Who has a pet mouse.

E is for Elephant
Who is so fat.

F is for Frog
Who wears a black hat.

Calum Adams (9)
St Mark's CE School, Brighton

Alphabet Poem

(An extract A - F)

A is for Andrew
Who breaks all the rules.

B is for Bob
Who has lots of tools.

C is for children
Who were playing in the house.

D is for David
Who has a pet mouse.

E is for Esme
Who always dyes her hair.

F is for Frog
Who got eaten by a bear.

Liam Terry (9)
St Mark's CE School, Brighton

Alphabet Poem

(An extract A - L)

A is for Andrew
Who has brown hair.

B is for Bethany
Who always wants to care.

C is for Calum
Who's always near.

D is for Dad
Who likes to drink beer.

E is for Esme
Who's always in a rush.

F is for Fred
Who likes his peas mushed.

G is for Gill
Who lives in America.

H is for Harry
Whose mum's called Erica.

I is for Ive
Who's always late.

J is for Janice
Who's always got mates.

K is for Kayleigh
Who's got a boat.

L is for Lily
Who's got a coat.

Nicole Waites (9)
St Mark's CE School, Brighton

Alphabet Poem

(An extract A - N)

A is for Ashley
Who brought a big sweet.

B is for Billy
Who has cheesy feet.

C is for Charlotte
Who always climbs walls.

D is for Dean
Who always falls.

E is for Emma
Who is really cheeky.

F is for Frances
Who is really sneaky.

G is for Georgia
Who loves to shop.

H is for Holly
Who is going to go pop.

I is for Isabelle
Who never stops talking.

J is for Jordan
Who really hates walking.

K is for Kayleigh
Who is always cheating.

L is for Lacey
Who never stops eating.

M is for Milly
Who makes lots of noise.

N is for Nicola
Who chases all the boys.

Lacey Cole (9)
St Mark's CE School, Brighton

Alphabet Poem

(An extract A - L)

A is for Alfie
Who always smells.
   A   B   C
B is for Betty
Who collects shells.
   A   B   C
C is for Claire
Who likes boys
   A   B   C
D is for Dan
Who makes lots of noise.
   A   B   C
E is for Emma
Who is really bad.
   A   B   C
F is for Fred
Who is always sad.
   A   B   C
G is for Georgia
Who likes to watch telly.
   A   B   C
H is for Hayley
Who likes strawberry jelly.
   A   B   C
I is for Ian
Who likes to play games.
   A   B   C
J is for Jackey
Who forgets names.
   A   B   C
K is for Kate
Who likes to shop.
   A   B   C
L is for Lily
Who likes to hop.
   A   B   C

Bethany Dahr (9)
St Mark's CE School, Brighton

Alphabet Poem
(An extract A - H)

A is for Andrew
Who plays with the rats.

B is for Bethany
Who keeps a cat.

C is for Chloe
Who is very shy.

D is for Daniel
Who is strong and never cries.

E is for Esme
Who plays in the park.

F is for Fred
Who is afraid of the dark.

G is for Gus
Who is rather smug.

H is for Harry
Who keeps a slug.

Peter Henderson (9)
St Mark's CE School, Brighton

Brighton Beach

The sun is glazing
On the beach it glitters
And shining on the sea.
The children paddling
On the shore
The wind is blowing on the shore.
The beautiful sea shining
Through the air.
Swift wind, all lovely and shiny,
Gorgeous glitters on the sea.

Anab Dahir (10)
St Mark's CE School, Brighton

Alphabet Poem

(An extract A - J)

A is for Andrew
Who breaks everyone's toys.

B is for Bethany
Who teases all the boys.

C is for Courtney
Who asks me for a fight.

D is for Dad
I see my dad every night.

E is for Esme
Who is a girl.

F is for Fred
Who rings the bell.

G is for Georgie
Who likes to play.

H is for Hollie
Who thinks it's a lovely day.

I is for Ivan
Who has no choice.

J is for Jasmine
Who has no voice.

Lily Mateer (9)
St Mark's CE School, Brighton

Brighton Seafront

Buildings high like 50 foot giants.
Windows watching three friends playing.
Arches are rainbows.
Bikes riding on the road
Carrying their heavy load.
Lamp posts stand tall
Talking to starlings.

Tia Riddle (11)
St Mark's CE School, Brighton

Brighton Beach

The sea spits on the shingle
It grabs stones and throws them in anger
Sun shines on the seashore
Creeping in more and more
All the shingle, boiling hot
Like the sun down low
Seaweed sways like an Hawaiian dancer
Sand sinks slowly
As the crabs crawl to the water's edge
Seashells sound like chimes
When pulled away by the furious sea.

Joanne Short (11)
St Mark's CE School, Brighton

Brighton Pier

The pier is like an old, rusty cooker
Creaking in the worst wind.
The sea is like a blue star on the floor
Twinkling in the sunlight.
Birds are like a hungry hunter
Looking for food.
The waves are like a mouth
Open for food.

Jay Gander (11)
St Mark's CE School, Brighton

Brighton Poem Of The Sea

The sea shifts towards the
Sunshine as the sun shines on me,
So I could float on the sea.

I walk across the sand as it
Feels like I'm walking on a hot
Desert as I sink in.

Alex Deacon (11)
St Mark's CE School, Brighton

The World In Brighton

Destructive waves crash,
A mighty Thor hurls lightning,
The great West Pier falls,
Aided by the howling wind,
Golden pavilion shines,
Heated sun brings colour from the gods,
Blue sky compresses its pain,
White clouds turn grey . . .
Nature wins again.

Nina Sarfas (11)
St Mark's CE School, Brighton

The Royal Pavilion

Palace damp with the dullness of darkness
Dazzling with dining diamonds
Chandeliers of destruction
Like the subtleness of the shining, shimmering sea
The silence of the city sleeping
Awakened by the proudness of her bold majesty
The regal jewel beckons our attention
Luminous amber reflecting off the velvet-black sky.

Sophie Joyce (11)
St Mark's CE School, Brighton

Brighton Pier

The sea is a river of water
A soft, calm piece of Heaven
The seashore shines
The seashore shimmers
It whistles in the wind
As the rusty pier fades in the darkness.

Connor Mateer (11)
St Mark's CE School, Brighton

Brighton Pavilion

Golden, shining in the face of darkness.
Golden, releasing its goodness to the soulless.
Golden, the palace and heart of glory.
Golden, shimmering across the water's edge revealing itself.
Golden, ricocheting gorgeous rays of golden sun.
Our world is falling deeper and deeper
Because of our terrible behaviour.
When will we find our golden saviour?
All alone, bare as the bone we moan, moan, moan!
The air isn't clear, we all shed a tear.
Golden, ultimate power reinforcing the kindness
We once all shared.
Golden, absorbing all the pain and hatred
Leaving it empty for all to start again.
Brighton, oh Brighton
Thank you.

Jamie Palmer
St Mark's CE School, Brighton

The Brighton Pavilion

Golden surprise,
Light from Heaven.
Crown for the king,
Spreading of fire.

Fighting of lights,
Thrown to be seen.
A castle of brightness,
A small breeze of wind.

Name to be proud of,
The darkened sky.
Symmetry reflections,
Light from a fairytale.

Danielle Anderson (11)
St Mark's CE School, Brighton

Pavilion Eyes

Amazing, amber, abstract palace
Reflecting royal regalness,
A small city
Lonely in madness
In cold, in heat,
Watch over us, pavilion eyes.
Reflecting royal regalness
Amazing, amber, abstract palace,
Like a star you can't reach
Small crystal,
With no mouth or hands.
Watch over us, pavilion eyes.
Amazing, amber, abstract palace
Reflecting royal regalness,
Like a stone to a beach,
Or a crown to a queen
With no food to eat.
Watch over us, pavilion eyes.
Reflecting royal regalness
Amazing, amber, abstract palace,
Tears without sadness
Heavens we dream of
With no fear of death.
Watch over us, pavilion eyes.
Watch over us!

Esme Sarfas (11)
St Mark's CE School, Brighton

Brighton Beach

Sea as blue as skies
A great blue whale
Seashells by the seashore
Crying salty tears as the rain falls.

Jessica Wilson
St Mark's CE School, Brighton

Brighton

Hear that sound
Come on down
To Brighton.

We see the pier
So we cheer
At Brighton.

Look! Candyfloss
How much? Gosh!
In Brighton.

Nicola Rosario (11)
St Mark's CE School, Brighton

Funky Monkey

There once was a little monkey
Who was quite a bit funky
He wanted to cry
But had no eye
Now he is a cheeky monkey.

Georgia Smith (10)
Telscombe Cliffs CP School, Peacehaven

Love Poem

I love Jack
Who has a cat that's black
I love Harry
Who I want to marry
I love Billy
Who loves me, Lilly.

Olivia Fisher (9)
Telscombe Cliffs CP School, Peacehaven

Horsey, Horsey

Horsey, horsey, let me ride you
Over the hills and far away
We can go clipty clop
Then trot
All the way to Three Greys Riding
I love riding!
I love horses!
I love working at Three Greys Riding!
It's more than fun!

Emma Brown (9)
Telscombe Cliffs CP School, Peacehaven

My Monkey

My monkey is furry
My monkey is brown
My monkey swings, bounces and springs
My monkey is happy
Sometimes sad
The more the happy
The more the glad.

Rebecca Mason (9)
Telscombe Cliffs CP School, Peacehaven

Snow, Snow

Snow, snow on the ground
Does not make a single sound.
Twinkling, shining and blue
Making the world look lovely and new.
Snow, snow on the ground
Does not make a single sound.

Hayley Clothier (9)
Telscombe Cliffs CP School, Peacehaven

The Senses

Are you in touch with your five senses?
Do you really try to keep them all alive
Or do you keep them sealed in a vase and not let them escape
Or do you stick them with bubblegum on your shoes?

Can you hear the screaming of the wind rattling the windows?
Can you hear the sizzling of the sausages in the saucepan?
Can you hear the birds chirping on a sunny morning
Or hear a coin plopping in a purse?

Can you taste the runny caramel and chocolate in your mouth?
Can you taste the apple pie and runny custard too?

Can you touch the autumn leaves upon the autumn trees
And maybe a breeze of autumn wind blowing in your face?

Can you smell the maple syrup on your scorching pancakes
Or maybe a piece of toffee roasting on your plate?

Can you see the clock strike ten on the grandmother clock
And see the pictures on your wall that bring joy to others' eyes?

So touch and taste and feel your life around you
And listen while you watch it unfold.

Hannah Tolley (8)
Telscombe Cliffs CP School, Peacehaven

The Senses

Are you in touch with each of your five senses?
Do you really try to keep them all alive
Or do you keep them down the toilet with the lid sealed shut?

Can you hear the car's engine revving?
Can you taste fizzy sweets on your tongue?
Can you touch a tree a metre away?
Can you smell my roast dinner?
Can you see eggs hatching?

So touch and taste and feel your life around you
And listen while you watch it all unfold.

Luke Harding (8)
Telscombe Cliffs CP School, Peacehaven

The Senses

Are you in touch with each of your five senses?
Do you really try to keep them all alive
Or do you keep them asleep, locked up in their metal cages
Asleep for all your life maybe?

Can you hear birds chirping on a sunny, Sunday morning?
Can you hear the splash when somebody has thrown a stone into
the sea?

Can you taste the spicy anger of when you have lost a battle with
your friends?

Can you touch the raindrops melting on your tongue?
Can you touch the soft petals of a rose?

Can you smell the sweet smelling of a rose?
Can you smell the salt from the sea?

Can you see the waves crashing up against the harbour wall?

So touch and taste and feel your life around you
And listen while you watch it all unfold.

Ria French (7)
Telscombe Cliffs CP School, Peacehaven

I Can Hear

I can hear the ghosts speaking
I can hear the wind whistling
I can hear the waves howling
I can hear the music playing
I can hear the balloons popping
I can hear the clock ticking
I can hear nothing
But me!

Charlotte Stuart (8)
Telscombe Cliffs CP School, Peacehaven

Alphabet Poem

A is for Alice who lives in Africa
Who sells apples to all the people around her.
B is for Bob who lives in Brighton
Who sells bananas to all the people around him.
C is for Cat who lives in Canada
Who sells carrots to all the people around her.
D is for Dan who lives in Disneyland
Who sells doughnuts to all the people around him.
E is for Elf who lives in Egypt
Who sells elephants to all the people around him.
F is for Fiona who lives in France
Who sells fairy cakes to all the people around her.
G is for George who lives in Greece
Who sells grapes to all the people around him.
H is for Hannah who lives in Hampshire
Who sells hotdogs to all the people around her.
I is for India who lives in Iceland
Who sells igloos to all the people around her.
J is for Jane who lives in Japan
Who sells jewels to all the people around her.
K is for Kevin who lives in Kingston
Who sells kites to all the people around him.
L is for Libby who lives in London
Who sells lights to all the people around her.
M is for Matthew who lives in Malta
Who sells matches to all the people around him.
N is for Natasha who lives in Newhaven
Who sells nets to all the people around her.
O is for Oliver who lives in Ottawa
Who sells oranges to all the people around him.
P is for Peter who lives in Paris
Who sells pigs to all the people around him.
Q is for Quinton who lives in Queensland
Who sells quilts to all the people around him.
R is for Rafe who lives in Rottingdean
Who sells rats to all the people around him.
S is for Scott who lives in Spain
Who sells sheep to all the people around him.

T is for Tracey who lives in Turkey
  Who sells tents to all the people around her.
U is for Ulrika who lives in the USA
  Who sells umbrellas to all the people around her.
V is for Victoria who lives in Venice
  Who sells vans to all the people around her.
W is for William who lives in Wales
  Who sells water to all the people around him.
X is for Xena who lives in Xar
  Who sells X-rays to all the people around her.
Y is for Yetta who lives in York
  Who sells yo-yos to all the people around her.
Z is for Zoe who lives in Zambia
  Who sells zips to all the people around her.

Libby Rose Luffingham (8)
Telscombe Cliffs CP School, Peacehaven

I Love To Dance!

When I dance I feel free as a bird.

I leap through the air and jump high in the sky,
Spinning round and round I feel like I can fly,
I twizzle and turn and go up on my toes,
Will the music stop? Nobody knows!

I see the people smiling,
From front row to back,
And when I finish dancing they all stand up
And clap!
It makes people happy and that feels great,
I love dancing so much but I wish I could skate!

Bethany Highsted (9)
Telscombe Cliffs CP School, Peacehaven

School

School, school, in the hall
Having assembly, coming out
Finding out what it's all about
Numeracy, literacy, having some fun
Doing PE in the beautiful sun
Break time, get out our snacks
While the teachers all relax
Science, history
Solving a mystery
Now it's the end of the day
So we can go home and play.

Faye Jones (9)
Telscombe Cliffs CP School, Peacehaven

Blue

Blue, blue, in the sky
Blue, blue, say goodbye
Blue, blue, in the air
Blue, blue, in your hair
Blue, blue, do the twist
Blue, blue, it's unfair
Blue, blue, in the clouds
Blue, blue kites.

Gabriella Siân Weston (9)
Telscombe Cliffs CP School, Peacehaven

My Twin

My twin is always there
She always tears my bear
And takes it to the fair
She never, ever cares
And sticks her bum in the air
Like she just doesn't care.

Jessica Spice (9)
Telscombe Cliffs CP School, Peacehaven

I Love Puppies

I love puppies
They are so cute
Some are huge
And some are minute
Puppies
Puppies
They are the best
Puppies
Puppies
They beat the rest
I lay them down
And tickle their tummies
And roll them over
And laugh, I think it's funny
I love puppies
Hooray!

Sharna Elise Vine (9)
Telscombe Cliffs CP School, Peacehaven

Summer

The sun is shining
Flowers are rising
Apples are red as roses.

Children playing in the sun
Laughter echoes of their fun.
Birds are nesting, chicks are born
Crops are growing, ripening corn.

Frogs are leaping, lambs are grazing
Farmers plough the fields.
Long summer nights for a walk
Of God's creations we will talk.

Daniel Tribe (8)
Telscombe Cliffs CP School, Peacehaven

My Poem

When I was one
I loved my mum.

When I was two
I started to chew.

When I was three
I jumped like a flea.

When I was four
I heard a knock on the door.

When I was five
I felt alive.

When I was six
I bought a Twix.

When I was seven
I was friends with Megan.

When I was eight
I broke a gate.

When I was nine
I sucked a lime.

When I was ten
I wrote this again.

Vanessa Tait (8)
Telscombe Cliffs CP School, Peacehaven

Homework

Homework is bad
Homework is sad
Homework is boring, it keeps me snoring
When I woke up my mum says to do it but I didn't want to
And she knew it
Homework is hard, I'd rather write a card
Homework is a menace, just like Dennis.

Connor Gaul (8)
Telscombe Cliffs CP School, Peacehaven

My Good Ten Years

When I was one
I had a big thumb.

When I was two
I went to the zoo.

When I was three
I fell off a tree.

When I was four
I fell through the floor.

When I was five
I was alive.

When I was six
I had a big chip.

When I was seven
I went to Heaven.

When I was eight
I had a big ape.

When I was nine
I was fine.

When I was ten
I read it again.

Mark Lee-Falcon (9)
Telscombe Cliffs CP School, Peacehaven

Ghost

Ghosts, pale and bloodless,
Gloomy, scary and frightful,
Their faces are spooky and grey.
Listen to the cry of the ghosts
As they hover by.
Stay still as they
Circle you and watch
Your every move.

Abigail Stuart (10)
Telscombe Cliffs CP School, Peacehaven

Senses

Are you in touch with all your five senses?
Do you really try to keep them all alive?

Can you hear the fairies' wings flapping in the breeze?
Can you hear the wind blowing through the trees?
Can you hear the birds cheeping each new morning
Or hear the seagulls talking?

Can you taste sweet, red strawberries?
Can you taste the butter in the buttercups?
Can you taste new grown cabbages
Or taste a ripe banana?

Can you touch the greenest leaves?
Can you touch a horse's mane?
Can you touch the light green grasshopper
Or touch a baby's toes?

Can you smell cookies cooling in the kitchen?
Can you smell the fresh air?
Can you smell sour lemons
Or smell sun-yellow daffodils?

Natasha Gravett (7)
Telscombe Cliffs CP School, Peacehaven

It

It's black and it's white
And it's sometimes grey,
It's dark on the walls and the floors.
It's quiet and silent
And follows you around
As it creeps over ceilings and doors.
Don't try and follow it, it follows you.

What is it?

A shadow!

Emilyn Louise Hulatt (10)
Telscombe Cliffs CP School, Peacehaven

Are You In Touch With Your Senses?

Are you in touch with each of your five senses?
Do you really try to keep them alive?
Do you keep them in a round, golden jar with the lid done up
And under your bed?

Can you hear the sound of golden, sparkly football boots
getting banged off and sharpened for his next game?

Can you taste brown chocolate biscuits being in your mouth,
all crispy and dry until it drops in your stomach?

Can you touch the leathery football with black squares all around
as you save it in the goal?

Can you smell perfume on your mum's dressing table
from your room when you are playing with your toys?

Can you see a boy playing rugby just behind the bush
that is green and when the wind blows it sort of waves at you?

So touch and taste and feel your life around you
And listen while you watch it all unfold.

Kevin Gunn (8)
Telscombe Cliffs CP School, Peacehaven

Wind On The Hill

No one can tell me,
Nobody knows
Where the wind goes.
It's flying from somewhere as fast as it can.
I couldn't keep up with it even if I ran.
But if I stopped holding the string of my kite.
It would fly away and it would be hard to get back.
So don't forget,
Where the wind goes is where the wind goes.

Bethany Yeates (9)
Telscombe Cliffs CP School, Peacehaven

My Sister Nat

Nasty Nat
Total brat
Backchat
Yip yap
Yahboo
Smack!
Take that!
Nasty Nat!

Nasty Nat
I call her fat
She hides in the attic
She's melodramatic
Smack!
That's my nasty Nat.

Connor McGill (9)
Telscombe Cliffs CP School, Peacehaven

The A-M Zoo

A family went to the zoo,
Boys, you can come too.
Can you see the tiger?
Did you see the cub beside her?
Elephants big and grey.
Frogs they all hop away.
Giraffes as tall as the sky.
Happy people all walk by.
I do like the zoo.
Jolly things to do.
Kicking a can on the floor.
Let's stay and do more.
Must we go? Goodbye.

Rhys Wheeler (10)
Telscombe Cliffs CP School, Peacehaven

Growing Up

When I was one
I liked my mum.

When I was two
What did you do?

When I was three
I saw a bee.

When I was four
I knocked at a door.

When I was five
I felt alive.

When I was six
I ate a Twix.

When I was seven
I went to Heaven.

When I was eight
I was very late.

When I was nine
Everything should have been mine.

When I was ten
I sat on a pen.

Sasha West (9)
Telscombe Cliffs CP School, Peacehaven

No Fear

No fear.
No fear.
I will be here.
The stars will be above,
So there will be no fear.
No fear.
I will stay with you.

Kim Bowles (9)
Telscombe Cliffs CP School, Peacehaven

Senses

Are you in touch with all your five senses?
Do you really try to keep them all alive?

Can you touch the baby's toes?
Can you touch a wild, red squirrel?
Can you touch a flower that has just bloomed
Or can you touch a fairy's wand?

Can you smell a fresh, turkey dinner?
Can you smell a rainbow?
Can you smell a butterfly far away
Or can you smell a white dove in a lake?

Can you taste the salty water in a shell?
Can you taste a daffodil?
Can you taste a glittery moon
Or can you taste the perfume in your nose?

Can you see a moon far away?
Can you see a silver reindeer?
Can you see a gold moon in the sky
Or can you see a lovely, sunny day?

Can you hear a spider spinning a web?
Can you hear a cloud float across the sky?
Can you hear a flower that's just bloomed
Or can you hear the raindrops on a rainbow?

So touch and feel your life around you
And listen while you watch it all unfold
And keep your senses all alive.

Luke Ashdown (8)
Telscombe Cliffs CP School, Peacehaven

The Twin

I've got a twin called Jessica
She sings in my ear like a parrot.
All she does is tear my bear,
Go to the fair and stick her bum up in the air.

Nataly Spice (9)
Telscombe Cliffs CP School, Peacehaven

Alphabet Poem

A little boy called Ben
B uilt a secret den
C ans were all over the floor
'D ear, dear,' said his mum through the door
'E mily wants to come in,' she said
'F orget it, I'm still in bed.'
'G et out of bed, Ben,
H urry up, it's half past ten.'
'I don't want to, I'm still sleepy.'
J ackie, his mum, just got weepy
K ate, his sister's friend
L ater is coming to lend
M onopoly, their favourite game
'N ow I've heard Kate's name
O f course I will get out of bed.'
'P lease hurry up,' his mum said
Q uite a few minutes later
R ushing in was Kate with an alligator
S houting, 'Come and see me!'
T ogether they had a cup of tea
U nder the teapot came a mouse
V anessa the cat chased it round the house
W hen Vanessa gobbled it up quickly
X -rays showed it was prickly
'Y ikes!' said Ben
'Z illions of pricks remind me of my pet hedgehog that died.'

Georgia Budd (9)
Telscombe Cliffs CP School, Peacehaven

Flowers

Flowers come in spring
In all types of colours
Like pink, purple and blue,
Orange, green and yellow
But the prettiest is red.

Rafe Hall (8)
Telscombe Cliffs CP School, Peacehaven

Dogs Poem

Dogs can be big, dogs can be small
But what we like about them is they're so cool.

Dogs can be fat, dogs can be thin
But what we don't like about them is they can let off a din.

Dogs can be happy, dogs can be sad
But we don't care because we know they are there.

Dogs, dogs everywhere
We love them and they really care.

Dogs don't like cats
And cats don't like dogs
But they get on together because we're around.

So when you get a dog don't be scared
Because they always love you and care.

Lianne Sullivan & Zoe Willard (8)
Telscombe Cliffs CP School, Peacehaven

It

It's black and it's tan and it's white with brown eyes.
It's jumpy and very cute.
It has a long tail with 4 bony legs,
It has very sharp teeth and you shouldn't give it a boot.

It has long, floppy ears and sharp, pointy claws.
It will always beg you for food.
It sleeps at the foot of your bed at night
And can put you in a bad mood.

It has a fur coat and is ever so soft.
It has a wet nose and long tongue.
It likes to drink water and tea.
Can you guess what it is?

(Answer - Dog)

Charly Letts (10)
Telscombe Cliffs CP School, Peacehaven

Angry Or Happy

When I am angry I am bad
When I am happy I am good.

When I am angry I throw my toys
When I am happy I pick them up.

When I am angry I ignore other people
When I am happy I help as much as I can.

It is good
To be happy.

Harry Wallace (9)
Telscombe Cliffs CP School, Peacehaven

Spring

Awake the flowers, come alive
Lovely flowers open wide.
The sun is shining and the flowers glisten
The silence . . . listen.

The trees grow long, tall and green
What a lovely, summery scene.
Lots of beauty in these plants we care for
But don't let children have them under four!

Hayley Greenfield (9)
Telscombe Cliffs CP School, Peacehaven

My Dog Sam

There once was a dog called Sam,
He'd love a piece of ham,
He'd love to play,
At the middle of the day,
That's my dog called Sam.

Dylan Brooks (7)
Telscombe Cliffs CP School, Peacehaven

I Love Sweets

I love
ice cream
but it will make me
scream.

I love
chocolate eggs
but they give me
wobbly legs.

I love
candyfloss
but it makes me
cross.

I love
wine gums
but they give me
a spotty bum.

I love
lollipops
but they give me
the chicken pox.

I love
toffee chunks
but they give me
the goosebumps.

I love
milkshakes
but they make my knees ache.

I love
liquorice sticks
but it makes me
sick!

I love
bubble gummy
but it makes me
go funny.

*But whatever
you do don't give
me jam tarts . . .*

Caiah Morash (9)
Telscombe Cliffs CP School, Peacehaven

The Waterfall

Calm, calm, getting a bit rough,
Getting bumpy.
It's coming, it's coming,
It's getting really bumpy.
Here comes the rocks.
Swosh, swosh!

I'm so excited
I can see it.
Here it comes,
5, 4, 3, 2, 1!
There it goes.
Ahh, weee, yahoo!
It's so bumpy.

It's coming to the big one.
Splash!
It's so white
And it's the end.
Waterfalls are such fun.

Eve Plumridge (9)
Telscombe Cliffs CP School, Peacehaven

Jungle Rumble

In the jungle you'll hear a sound.
It will give you a fright yet it will be loud.
The ground will rumble.
The rocks will tumble.
The trees will shiver.
The leaves will quiver
As you meet Lion River.

In the jungle you'll find a man.
He will seem quite strange talking to a tin can.
He will be quite weird
With his tangled, old beard.
You will hear him mumble
When he is in the rainy jungle.

You'll find a monkey hanging
And an elephant banging.
The tiger will leap
And the lizard will creep.
The gorilla will eat meat.

What else lies in the deep?

Harry Norman & Adam Leadbitter (9)
Telscombe Cliffs CP School, Peacehaven

River

Bubble maker,
Wave shaker,
Lovely sparkler,
Crash happener,
Happy bubble,
Rainbow lover,
Star reflector,
Excellent looker.
What am I?

(Answer - River)

Laura Holland (10)
Telscombe Cliffs CP School, Peacehaven

The School Dinner Poem

I don't like school dinners
They are always out of date.
The carrots are burnt
The chips are dirt
And always make me late.

I don't like school dinners
They always make me shiver.
They give me eyes
And brain
And sometimes give me liver.

I don't like school dinners
They always make me scream.
They always give me Brussels
But never strawberry cream.

Ellie Brown (9)
Telscombe Cliffs CP School, Peacehaven

The Listeners

'Is anybody in?' said the knight in white
Banging on the iron door
And his horse in the darkness paced the pathway
Of the house's stone floor
And a snake slipped out of the letterbox
Level with his knees
And slithered away in the moonlight
To the safety of the trees
But no one descended to the knight
No face looked out from the darkened sill
And met with his pale blue eyes
Where he stood puzzled and still.

Daniel Coster (9)
Telscombe Cliffs CP School, Peacehaven

Summer

The air is warm,
the sky is bright.
I like to drink lots of Sprite.

The sunshine is hot,
the sunshine is burning
and while that's happening, the Earth is turning.

I'm at the fair,
I'm brushing my hair.
The candy's sweet,
the birds go tweet!

It's time to close,
I do a pose
and say thank you for looking after us.

Senne Porter (7)
Telscombe Cliffs CP School, Peacehaven

A Sea Poem

The reflective water collects
and the rock-pushing wave
expands.
The rocks tumble as the
wave starts to curl.
The surfers are ready,
ready for the tube.
It's nerve-wracking,
it's exhilarating,
it's a surfer's dream.

Mitchell Hall (10)
Telscombe Cliffs CP School, Peacehaven

The Sweetest Thing

The sweetest thing is like a rose
Or when the scent of lavender reaches your nose
It could be a romantic letter
Or maybe something even better
A trip to the beach
Is not out of reach
With the sun and the sand
You both sit hand in hand
Or maybe going to the cinema is best
Where you can sit, relax and rest
There you sit side by side
And as much as you've tried
You still can't find the sweetest thing
It may be the presents that you bring
Or maybe, just maybe, a romantic white dove
But no, the sweetest thing, is love.

Jessica Newman (11)
Telscombe Cliffs CP School, Peacehaven

Limericks

There was a young man from Dundee
Whose cat jumped up an oak tree
He started to scream
But it was a dream
That silly, young man from Dundee.

There was a man from a strange land
Who liked making things out of sand
And he was the best
He had tons of guests
This man from a very strange land.

Hannah Vicary (10)
Telscombe Cliffs CP School, Peacehaven

School Dinners

I do not like school dinners,
They are always very poor,
They always make me feel sick,
I shout, 'I don't want any more!'

I do not like school dinners,
The toast is covered in hairs,
The plate is always dirty
And no one actually cares!

Oliver Knights (9)
Telscombe Cliffs CP School, Peacehaven

I'll Give You . . .

I'll give a stick of glue
Maybe a marshmallow or two.
I'll give you a hose
Stick it up your nose.
It goes to your brain,
You start to get pain,
Before you know it
It's lunchtime again.

Jack Prout (9)
Telscombe Cliffs CP School, Peacehaven

Ghosts Go By

Silently, silently, your mouth goes dry.
Shudder, shake and tremble.
Be quiet, be still, as the ghosts float by.
Pale, transparent, shimmering and moaning.
Empty, dark and dead,
They yell, bellow and shudder then sigh.
Be still as the ghosts float by.

Lauren Brooks (9)
Telscombe Cliffs CP School, Peacehaven

Jazz Friends

Jazz friends
Animals friends
Seashore friends
Special friends.

Forever friends
Rear friends
Icky friends
Enjoyable friends
Nasty friends
Dirty friends
Spoilt friends.

Shelby Collins (9)
Telscombe Cliffs CP School, Peacehaven

The Cat

The cat
had a bat
and he sat
on the mat.
He even had
a cap
a blue mouse too
with a shoe.

Francesca Jewell (8)
Telscombe Cliffs CP School, Peacehaven

Love

Our love is like a golden chain,
It binds two hearts together
And if you ever broke that chain,
You'd break my heart
Forever!

Kaya Edwards (10)
Telscombe Cliffs CP School, Peacehaven

Alphabet Poem

A river's here,
B ubbling near,
C ascading through the grass.
D ucks all over,
E ven in the clover,
F orgetting all bad thoughts.
G ushing down,
H igh and round,
I n and out of tunnels.
J ogging through meanders,
K eeping behind banners,
L ovely rivers flow.
M oving nice and lush,
N ever in a rush,
O ver, under they go.
P ebbles under the river,
Q uietly they quiver,
R ough and sometimes calm.
S plashing water,
T hat won't alter,
U nderneath the lakes.
V ivid and cold,
W ater's bold,
X -raying the fish.
Y awn! That's a lot of writing,
Z zzzzz! Can someone turn out the lighting!

Abigail Padgham (10)
Telscombe Cliffs CP School, Peacehaven

Old Man From Spain

There once was an old man from Spain
Who suffered from dreadful back pain
He went to a doc
Who gave him a shock
And cured was that old man from Spain.

Laura Clothier (10) & Ellen Hunt (9)
Telscombe Cliffs CP School, Peacehaven

Alphabetical Poem

A ngela was very sad
B ecause the sky was weary and grey.
C louds filled the sky.
D own came the rain.
E verything got soaked.
F ather came into the room.
'G o and get your paints,'
H e said.
'I will,' said Angela.
J ust then the doorbell rang.
K elly had come round to play.
'L et her in,' said dad.
M um was doing the cooking.
N ow it's time to bake the cakes.
'O pen the oven door,
P lease, Angela.'
Q uickly she opened the door.
R oaring heat came out of the oven.
'S mells lovely,' said Kelly.
T iggy the cat came into the kitchen.
U nder the table the fat cat went.
'V ery cute cat,' said Kelly.
'W ill you stay for tea?' said mum.
X ylophones played on the radio.
'Y es, please,' said Kelly.
'Z ebras are very stripy,' said Angela.

Melissa Camp (9)
Telscombe Cliffs CP School, Peacehaven

My Little Dog!

We saw a little dog,
Who wanted to play with frog.
He started to jump
But landed with a bump
Now he has a lump.

Amy Barnard (10)
Telscombe Cliffs CP School, Peacehaven

Animals Around The World

In the Arctic, in the Arctic,
Cold-hearted Arctic fox,
Gliding fish, gliding fish,
Long term swimming Polar bear,
Diving penguins, diving penguins.

In the jungle, in the jungle,
Tigers prowl in the undergrowth,
Monkeys swing, monkeys swing,
Colourful parrots fly around,
Lizards climb, lizards climb.

In the desert, in the desert,
Camels wander the scorching land,
Kangaroos hop, kangaroos hop,
Meerkats scuttle down their holes,
Flamingos stand, flamingos stand.

On the Plains, on the Plains,
Long-necked creatures eat the leaves,
Lions roar, lions roar,
Gazelles are hopping all around,
Elephants thud, elephants thud.

In the woods, in the woods,
Bears patrol around all day,
Eagles soar, eagles soar,
Wolves howl at the moon,
Hawks hunt, hawks hunt.

Now we are home, now we are home,
Cats purring on the rug,
Canaries cheep, canaries cheep,
Dogs are barking at my legs,
Hamsters sleep, hamsters sleep.

Alexandra Hanscomb & Catherine Dawkins (11)
Telscombe Cliffs CP School, Peacehaven

Roses Are Red, Violets Are Blue

Roses are red, violets are blue,
I like school, I hope you do too.
Roses are red, violets are blue,
cats are funny, so are you.
Roses are red, violets are blue,
dogs are mad, I know you are too.
Roses are red, violets are blue,
you think I'm mad, look at you.

Roses are red, violets are blue,
I hate poo, what about you?
Roses are red, violets are blue,
cats are stupid, you are too.
Roses are red, violets are blue,
dogs are spotty, so are you.
Roses are red, violets are blue,
fish are cute, it's true.

Roses are red, violets are blue,
Chloe is bonkers, but so am I.
Roses are red, violets are blue,
I might be crazy, well look at you.
Roses are red, violets are blue,
I have the best teacher in the world.
Roses are red, violets are blue,
baby fish are like fireballs racing towards the Earth.

Roses are red, violets are blue,
Emma is mad, mad as can be.
Roses are red, violets are blue,
Miss A Pronger is the best of them all.
Roses are red, violets are blue,
Chloe is as funny, as funny can be.
Roses are red, violets are blue,
my mum's loving as can be.

Pia Brice (11)
Telscombe Cliffs CP School, Peacehaven

Pets

A dog would be nice
But think of the price
Can't have one.
Dad said, 'Son
Even though you want one
Forget it, son.
Get a mouse
Have it in the house
In its cage
Jumping in rage
Kipping in its hay
Lazing all day.'
Maybe a mouse would be okay!

Ryen Teague (9)
Telscombe Cliffs CP School, Peacehaven

River

Reflection maker
Wave chaser
Sea finder
Rushing rapids
Frothy waterfall
Boat carrier
Fishes' home
Sun attracter
Greeny ocean
Clear blue streams
Bubbly white horses
Calm rainbow shines down
My journey has finished.

Sophie Peters (9)
Telscombe Cliffs CP School, Peacehaven

A Dream

We have
Long dreams,
Short dreams,
Very, very tall dreams,
Some are fat dreams,
Some are thin dreams
But I like the ever, everlasting ones
So I don't have to go to school.

Nikki Moore (8)
Telscombe Cliffs CP School, Peacehaven

The River

The calm, calm river floats slowly along
reflecting the burning sun
on its glistening surface.
Far ahead lies a fall
turning the calm, calm river into mist
smashing against the solid, grey rocks
at the bottom.

David Vance (10)
Telscombe Cliffs CP School, Peacehaven

The Feel Poem

I feel bad when I'm sad
Because people make fun of me
And when people make
Me happy I am glad.
When people make me angry
I am really mad,
When I'm embarrassed.

Roland Beshong (9)
Telscombe Cliffs CP School, Peacehaven

Alphabet Poem
(An extract A - M)

A small and furry dog
B rown and white
C an't see him when he is hiding
D anny was his name
E verywhere he goes, he follows his owner
F red, Fred runs round the park and in his
G arden with his dog Danny.
H urry, Danny
I t's getting dark
J ust as the dark clouds filled the sky he
K ept chasing windswept
L eaves before
M oving swiftly home to cuddle up next to the fire with his master.

Bethan Hoad (9)
Telscombe Cliffs CP School, Peacehaven

My Alphabet Poem
(An extract A - M)

A ll at once I saw a cat
B ut I couldn't believe how fat
C urling up fast asleep
D oing what cats do, what a treat
E vening comes, want to stray
F oraging in the night-time grey
G etting fatter day by day
H oping for food and no woes
I nto the darkness that lasts
J ust to belong to those who are older
K illing is a natural obsession
L ike sleeping is a natural succession
M e, I am a simple pussycat.

Gemma Heyes (9)
Telscombe Cliffs CP School, Peacehaven

Alphabet Poem

A ginger, furry cat saw a
B all of white string
C hased it this way and that
D own the road
E ven up the street
F lowers everywhere
G rocer stall too
H at stand, crash, big splash
I nk everywhere
J eronimo
K ings here dash
L ion run!
M itzy! Mitzy!
N aughty Mitzy
O ut of control
P urring princess
Q ueen of all cats
R uling her empire
S *top! Stop!*
T omcat, handsome tomcat
U ntil now nothing has stopped her
V ernon stares
W ith bulgy eyes
X -ray eyes scan the beauty in front of him
Y ou are the only cat for me
Z est fills my heart.

Gabriella Shuttleworth (10)
Telscombe Cliffs CP School, Peacehaven

Haiku

The leaves are so brown
In the dark and scary woods
The floor is bumpy.

Emily Blake (10)
Telscombe Cliffs CP School, Peacehaven

Alphabet Poem

A big, fluffy dog goes to a zoo
B efore he chased a
C at down the scary
D ark alleyway, he heard an
E eeeek! Eeeeek! It was a
F unky rat feeling a bit
G roovy. 'Will you break my
H eart?' said the rat
I nstinctively. 'Are you
J oking?' said the dog.
'K iss me, you
L ousy but
M agnificent dog.'
'N o, why should I kiss a sewer rat?'
'O h, you don't love me
P lease go out with me
Q uickly, come this way I can hear a
R abbit.'
'S hut up, I can't hear anything but
T rees swaying
U nder the atmosphere
V iolins
W ith xylophones.'
'Y ou have rubbish hearing, dog. Oh no, here comes a
Z ebra.'

Adam Docherty (10)
Telscombe Cliffs CP School, Peacehaven

The Snail

There once was a foolish snail
Who always looked like he was pale
He sat on a stick
He never got hit
But then he lost his tail.

Sophie Goujon (10)
Telscombe Cliffs CP School, Peacehaven

Alphabet Poem

A ginger kitten called Tigger
B ecame bigger and bigger
C omes round to see me every day
D ashing around in the hay
E ven though she lives next door
F urry, stripy, cute, she wiggles her paw
G inger beauty, can this be true?
H ad to play with me and you
 I n my window she would jump
J ust to see me and my dog called Trump
K itty, kitty, I love you so
L ove to see you grow and grow
M iaow, miaow, she would sing
N ow I can see how much joy you bring
O n my lap you would sit and purr
P urr, purr, purr, I stroke your fur
Q uick as a flash she darts about
R ound and round, *'Tigger!'* I shout
S top and sit back on my lap
T o have a cuddle and a nap
U nder the table, scared she is now
V illage cats attack her and prowl
W ith my hand I shoo them away
X -ray is ordered on kitty this day
Y ou are alright, thank goodness for that
Z ooming around, now a beautiful cat!

Megan Parsons (10)
Telscombe Cliffs CP School, Peacehaven

The Funky Monkey

There once was a funky monkey,
Who was very, very chunky,
He jumped off a tree
And bounced up past Lee
And landed in the tree again.

Harry Brooks (10)
Telscombe Cliffs CP School, Peacehaven

My Imaginary Dog

My imaginary dog
Is someone you love.
He tugs, he pulls,
He gives you huge hugs.

My imaginary dog
Is a spaniel.
I was thinking
His name could be Daniel.

My imaginary dog
Is fiction no more
But the money I've spent on him
Made me so poor!

Megan Taylor (9)
Telscombe Cliffs CP School, Peacehaven

The Vampire's Bat

The vampire's bat
Comes out at night,
He will suck your
Blood if you go in his sight.
Every night he has a drink of blood,
He will get you in your window at night.
If you lock the window,
He will smash your window
In a big fright,
Then the bat flies
To the gory tree of death.
When he gets there
He will turn into a vampire.

Louis Bywaters (9)
Telscombe Cliffs CP School, Peacehaven

Down The Pier

A beautiful day in summer
B right and sunny and clear
C hristian and James, his brother
D awdled down to the pier.
E verything they tried was fun
F rom slot machines to ghost train rides
G reat big ice creams melting in the sun
H aving fun at the seaside.
I n their bags they lugged on their backs
J affa cakes, bananas and sandwiches too
K ids crowded round the racing car track
L ate comers join the queue.
M edals and certificates given out to you
N aughty little children running around
'O i you, give me back my shoe!'
P eople making all kinds of sounds.
Q uad bikes roaring round the pier
R ight back to the beginning again
S eagulls swooping, coming very near
T he evening show features a dame.
U nder a canopy the old man draws
V arious people and their features
W hen all of a sudden a dog with black paws
X avier with a teacher
Y anks his master into the water
Z oom, zoom back to the shore - to meet up with his daughter.

Jeremy Saunders (10)
Telscombe Cliffs CP School, Peacehaven

Horses Of The Waves

The white horses of waves
Run with the tide
As they fall, more approach the shore
Where muzzles and shimmering white bodies slowly fall
And they crash on the pebbles of the beach.

Frankie White (10)
Telscombe Cliffs CP School, Peacehaven

Jake

There once was a boy called Jake
Who sat on a big, sharp rake
He got off his butt
And he saw a red cut
And he shouted, 'For goodness sake!'
The next day something else happened to Jake . . .
And this is going to make you hungry.

There once was a boy called Jake
Who sat on a creamy cake
He ran to his mum
And he showed her his bum
And she said, 'I'll scrape it off with flake.'
Another thing happened to Jake . . .

There once was a boy called Jake
Who was turned into a scary snake
He hissed at everyone
He hissed at his mum
And she hit him with a rake.
The end . . . ha, ha!

Lewis Mitchell (10)
Telscombe Cliffs CP School, Peacehaven

The Ghost

Silently hovering over soft carpets,
Floating through walls,
Frightening is his job,
Never will he stop.
Transparent, pale and white
Is his colour.
He moves things without a sound.

Shaylea Merrick (10)
Telscombe Cliffs CP School, Peacehaven

Alphabet Poem

A frica is far away
B aboons play happily all day
C alling birds are in the trees
D rifting on the silent breeze
E choes of thunder are in the sky
F rightening lightning screeches by
G orillas stopping for a rest
H ave just one day to build a nest
 I n the middle of the night
J ungle insects crawl and bite
K ing of the jungle with his pride
L ions are walking side by side
M onkeys swing from branch to branch
N ever fall and like to dance
O n the river tribesmen row
P iranhas swim deep below
Q uick as a flash the cheetah
R acing along his prey he knows
S nakes on a mission to find a frog
T akes position by a log
U nder the trees, near the top
V iviparous lizards never stop
W hen night-time falls the glow-worms light
X -rays in hospitals aren't as bright
Y et another day has passed in the depths of the jungle.
Z zzzzzzzzz.

Jack Cooper (9)
Telscombe Cliffs CP School, Peacehaven

Roses

Roses pretty nice
Ouch the thorn
Seedling born
Cut them for a special night.

Lauren Rose Stunell (10)
Telscombe Cliffs CP School, Peacehaven

The Horse Ride

A fter the rain,
B lue sky came out.
C atch the mane!
D on't shout!
E mpty the lane,
F orget that pout.
G o again.
H elp! Don't doubt,
I njuries cause pain,
J ust mount.
K een, that Jane
L ook about,
M ove around and get that rein.
N ag alert,
O pen the gate,
P rick her ears up,
Q uick, don't be late.
R eady?
S addle up,
T ake the strain,
U p and over,
V ery good, back down the lane.
W atch her walk around about,
eX perience takes the rein.
Y elling, 'There's that lout.'
Z oom, the horse is gone again.

Kellyann Davies (10)
Telscombe Cliffs CP School, Peacehaven

The Ghost

The ghost hovers and glides through walls.
The ghost moans for its life badly
The ghost feels sad at its death.
The ghost is unseen and transparent.
The ghost drifts from each house to scare.

Gabriella Cox (10)
Telscombe Cliffs CP School, Peacehaven

Alphabet Poem

A nimals are all different shapes and sizes
B unnies are often given as prizes
C ats like sleeping at home
D ogs like chewing on a bone
E lephants are big
F ish are small
G iraffes have long necks which make them look tall
H orses like to run
I nsects can be quite fun
J oeys can be quite funny
K angaroos keep them in their tummy
L ions roam free
M onkeys swing from tree to tree
N ewts like swimming together
O nly in the sunny weather
P igeons love to eat bread
Q uick, run, before they land on your head
R ats are small and creep about
S ewers are where rats hang out
T en minutes ago I didn't know what to do
U ntil I wrote this poem for you
V ictoria is a monkey ready for bed
W ith her brother and sister they have just been fed
X marks the spot where animals belong
Y ou can tell by the very bad pong
Z zzzzz – Victoria snoring in her bed.

Victoria Collings (10)
Telscombe Cliffs CP School, Peacehaven

Motorbikes

Motorbikes go broom, broom, broom
Motorbikes are very fast
Motorbikes look really cool
And mine's brand new.

Ashley Mark Derrick (9)
Telscombe Cliffs CP School, Peacehaven

Ziggy The Guinea Pig

A small and furry guinea pig,
B egan to dig a hole,
C harging up and down,
D igging like a mole,
E ating all the things he had,
F inding some taste good, some bad,
G oing down the hole he dug,
H aving it get very snug,
I t seemed a bit of a silly task,
J ust to dig and get nowhere fast,
K eeping sight of the piece of light,
L ight to guide him getting bright,
M oving slowly to the end,
N ow he sees the tunnel bend,
O nly now can he go fast,
P ushing through the lump of grass,
Q uite so bright he did not think,
R eally, so it makes him blink,
S o happy he was to be out,
T hirsty he came about,
U p to the water bowl,
V ery sad there was a hole,
W ater there was not,
eX cept for his pot,
Y es, the smelly old guinea pig was tame,
Z iggy was his name.

Kristy Lewis (10)
Telscombe Cliffs CP School, Peacehaven

The Moon

Moon, moon
Shine so bright
In the night
Like a light.

Jamie Gardner (9)
Telscombe Cliffs CP School, Peacehaven

Weeping Willow

(This is a poem about an 11-year-old girl whose best friend dies)

Weeping willow with your tears running down,
Why do you always weep and frown?
Is it because he left you one day?
Is it because he could not stay?
On your branches he would swing,
Do you long for the happiness that day would bring?
He found shelter in your shade,
He thought his laughter would never fade.
Weeping willow, stop your tears,
There is something to calm your fears.
You think death has forever ripped you apart
But I know
He'll always be in your heart.
When you think he's gone somewhere dull
Just look deep down into your soul.

Rebecca Seabrook & Megan Horscraft (11)
Telscombe Cliffs CP School, Peacehaven

Poems

I love poems
That focus on one thing
Like cats, dogs and mice
And words that go ka-ching!

I love poems
Most of them rhyme
Some of them don't
But I still think they're spectacular!

I love poems
I've put some in a book
They're so great that
People want a look!

Kelsey Welch (10)
Telscombe Cliffs CP School, Peacehaven

Dog Mayhem

A big, black dog named Fred
Barked before I went to bed.
'Cut that out!'
Dad began to shout.
'End the shouting,' said mum
Falling on her bum
Getting in the way of the cat
He was sitting on the mat.
I began to laugh.
'Just get in that bath.'
Karen, my sister, began to cry.
Liam, my brother, he dashed by.
Mum said, 'That dog's got to go.'
No! we all yelled. *No, no, no!*
Oh but he's got to stay.
Please, he likes to play.
'Quiet, you lot!' said dad
Rattling Fred's lead because he looked sad.
'See now, Mum, he won't bark anymore.'
The family let Fred out the door.
Up the park we all went to play.
We smiled at each other, we knew he could stay.

Liam Hannigan (10)
Telscombe Cliffs CP School, Peacehaven

A Man From Japan

There was an old man,
He came from Japan,
With a fantastic suntan,
He ate from a saucepan,
Drank from a can,
Oh, isn't he a funny, old man,
All the way from Japan.

Michelle Hills (8)
West Blatchington Junior School, Hove

Modern Train

Like a falcon catching its prey
As it soars in the air on a sunny day
It swoops down like an eagle
As they enter a tunnel of ebony darkness
Faces reflect in the total darkness
It speeds along, bumping, spinning, making a song
The track is brown, the train is green
As it chugs along with a lovely song
As it puffs along all past the meadow
Alongside are the horse and cattle
It glides swiftly along like a memory of the past
Swaying and lurching, travelling fast.

Sam McCormick (9)
West Blatchington Junior School, Hove

Skeletons In The Graveyard

Clinking, clanking skeletons revive
Slowly stretching and coming alive.

Bony fingers creeping through the ground
Coming through, making no sound.

Inscriptions on the gravestone saying
Leave the dead alone!

Eerie and silent, still at night
Only go in the graveyard at light.

Slowly the bodies move around
Leaping, creeping, making no sound.

Ben McCormick (8)
West Blatchington Junior School, Hove

Moods Of The Sea

As I lay on the warm sand, it feeds my body like a fuel
The sun shines like a crown jewel.
The sapphire sky surrounds me in haze,
As I lay drinking in the sea in a daze.
The sea is calm like a dove,
It makes me feel enveloped with love.
The sun reflects in the turquoise space,
I can feel the rays burning on my face.

The sea crashed against the rocks,
I could feel the cold wind right through my socks.
The rain makes me sad,
The thunder makes me mad.
When the sea is so rough,
I feel everything but tough.
The sand is now cold,
I have nothing to hold.

Rebekah Elphick (10)
West Blatchington Junior School, Hove

Ocean Dreams

Dolphins spray water in my face,
when they glide in water with grace.
When my mind swirls around,
so do the dolphins swimming round.
Their eyes always seem to gleam with pride,
whenever we swim side by side.

They come from far and wide in the sun,
to jump in front of boats just for fun.
I think of them every second of the day,
because they're always there ready to play.
Wherever we swim we are free,
that's as good as life can be.

Shannon Brown (10)
West Blatchington Junior School, Hove

People

Some people are black,
Some people are white,
Some people are bad
But some are alright!

Some people are yellow,
Other people are brown,
Some people smile a lot
While some people frown!

People, people, everywhere.
Some people just don't care!
I hope that I'm a person who does care
About people, people, everywhere!

Stephanie Batts   (7)
West Blatchington Junior School, Hove

The Mermaid

A mermaid sat on
a sandy rock,
as her eyes beamed,
'Come with me,' she called,
'I'll take you away to the land
beneath the sea.

We'll ride on dolphins,
we'll play with whales,
eat kelp for our tea
and swim
and be free.'

Rahima Begum   (10)
West Blatchington Junior School, Hove

Jasmine Jingelberry

Jasmine Jingelberry is a new girl at our school,
She always makes up the rule.

She has long, ginger hair,
Which burns like a flame in the air.

Her boots are twisted and black,
Which makes you want to attack.

Her ears stand out,
And sway about.

They flap out like a bird's wing,
She also loves to sing.

Wailing and failing, losing the note,
She never wins the classes' vote.

I made up my choice,
I love that voice.

She's the girl for me,
That's all that's said to be.

Lucy Bone (9)
West Blatchington Junior School, Hove

The Bizzie Train

Here is a train speeding along
Bumping and spinning and making a song
Childhood memories whistle by
Hitting the fireworks as they fly
Faster than a cheetah catching its prey
Whizzing through a sheltered bay
The ride is over
People stop and stare
As it starts again and no one knows where.

Ayesha Begum (9)
West Blatchington Junior School, Hove

Sam

Sam is my dog, he's a very silly dog.
He chases rabbits when we take him for a walk.
He puffs and pants on hot, sunny days
And he dances with my dad on a Sunday.
He loves Tiggi my cat
And she loves him back,
Rubbing up and purring,
He likes to sniff her back.
Sam runs round the garden, chasing wasps and flies,
When he manages to catch one
Sam coughs and nearly dies!

Kimberley Holdaway (8)
West Blatchington Junior School, Hove

The Arena Of Destruction

Crazy Mazy has to see Fisty Misty
In the destruction final.
Shall she win or shall she lose
In this fight for World Idol?
Crazy Mazy picks up Fisty Misty.
Fisty Misty screams in pain
While Crazy Mazy does it again.
Fisty Misty tries to break free
But Crazy Mazy hits her with her knee.
Fisty Misty lands on the floor
She can't fight any more.
Crazy Mazy, winner of World Idol 2004.

Lee Rebbeck (7)
West Blatchington Junior School, Hove

Cats And Dogs

Cats are small, some dogs big,
Cats and dogs like to dig.
Dogs like to go for a walk,
For the toilet and to talk.
Cats lay and play all day long,
Like to miaow like a song.
Some, I think, would try to bite
But I think that they're all right.
They make good house pets and treat you right.
Dogs are good guard dogs, got good sight.
Cats might try but have no might.
So at the end you can see
All the goodness and happiness they bring to you and me.
As it's for you to see.

Sara Gurcuoglu (9)
West Blatchington Junior School, Hove

Bed In Summer

In winter I get up at night
And dress by yellow candlelight.
In summer, quite the other way,
I have to go to bed by day.

I have to go to bed and see
The birds still hopping on the tree,
Or hear the grown-up people's feet
Still going past me in the street.

And does it not seem hard to you
When all the sky is clear and blue
And I should like so much to play
To have to go to bed by day?

Hayley Greco (9)
West Blatchington Junior School, Hove

The Brighton Play-Offs

There are two legs, one home and one away,
That's two games for Brighton to play.
I went on a coach with my mum,
We shouted, 'Come on, come on, come on come.'
It was a tough match but we won
Because Brighton are the number one.

I hoped we'd win the home game.
It was exciting, we sat in the rain.
Swindon were playing very well.
I think we had a magic spell
Because we scored in the last minute.
I thought perhaps we could win it!

'Penalties!' I was a bit scared
But I think Brighton were prepared.
We won and are going to Cardiff,
I wonder if we'll win, *if, if, if . . .?*
Good luck, team, especially goalie Ben,
Then I can say *when, when, when?*

Syd Wilson (8)
West Blatchington Junior School, Hove

The Stars

Stars, stars, flying in the sky
The stars are floating way up high
Touching the dark blue sky
It almost looks like they can fly
The stars come out at night
They make a very bright light.

Sandra Sidarous (8)
West Blatchington Junior School, Hove

Football Mad

I love to play football
It's the best game in the world
There's no other game like it
And it can be played by boys and girls.

When I play in attack
It's such a great feeling
When I've managed to score a goal
And to hear the crowd cheering.

I celebrate like mad
And slide along in the dirt
I love to get muddy
But I hate to get hurt!

Adam Mates (8)
West Blatchington Junior School, Hove

Flowers

Flowers are red
Flowers are blue
Flowers are all colours
So are you.

Are you in love?
If you are tell me now
I will buy you some flowers
In all sorts of colours.

Emma Perry (8)
West Blatchington Junior School, Hove